UNDERSTANDING
THE MASS MEDIA

UNDERSTANDING THE MASS MEDIA

A practical approach for teaching

BY

NICHOLAS TUCKER

CAMBRIDGE
AT THE UNIVERSITY PRESS
1967

CAMBRIDGE UNIVERSITY PRESS
Cambridge, New York, Melbourne, Madrid, Cape Town, Singapore, São Paulo, Delhi

Cambridge University Press
The Edinburgh Building, Cambridge CB2 8RU, UK

Published in the United States of America by Cambridge University Press, New York

www.cambridge.org
Information on this title: www.cambridge.org/9780521111966

© Cambridge University Press 1966

First published 1966
Reprinted with corrections 1967
This digitally printed version 2009

A catalogue record for this publication is available from the British Library

Library of Congress Catalogue Card Number: 65-14343

ISBN 978-0-521-06654-9 hardback
ISBN 978-0-521-11196-6 paperback

*To Jacqueline and
Mathew, with love*

CONTENTS

ACKNOWLEDGEMENTS

Apart from the works quoted in the text, it will be obvious to any reader that I have been particularly influenced by the work of Richard Hoggart and Raymond Williams, as well as by Denys Thompson and F. R. Leavis's pioneering work, *Culture and Environment*. With these, I would also like to thank the Society for Education in Film and Television and the Advertising Inquiry Council for the immense help I have had from their practical work over the years, and I would strongly recommend these two excellent services to any teacher interested in the mass media. I have always found very stimulating the quarterly *Use of English*, published by Chatto and Windus and edited by Denys Thompson; by far the best introduction to the practical teaching of English I know. Messrs Hall and Whannel allowed me to look at their stimulating and provocative work *The Popular Arts* while still in manuscript, and for this too I am extremely grateful.

I would also like to thank Mr Peter Vansittart, my first and best English teacher, Mr Richard Layard, who first gave me the idea of writing this book, Mr Tony Hodgkinson, from whom I have learned a great deal about films, Miss Frances Welch, for sharing with me her vast knowledge of popular music, and my brother Andrew for his extremely useful assistance. It is also a pleasure to be able to thank the staff and pupils of the two comprehensive schools where I taught for their patience and support during the time I was first experimenting with some of these ideas. The staff, too, of the Cambridge University Press have helped with the preparation of this book; the faults that remain are of course entirely my own.

N.T.

INTRODUCTION

In October 1960 the National Union of Teachers organised a conference on 'Popular Culture and Personal Responsibilities', where representatives from education and the mass media met and considered their different points of view. The educationalists tended to blame the providers for the low standard of their products; the providers, who in this case represented the B.B.C., I.T.V. and the *Daily Mirror*, replied that they were merely giving the public what it wanted, and if the level of appreciation was low, the fault lay with the teachers. One educationalist who disagreed with the providers was Jack Longland, director of education for Derbyshire.

'What is the good of trying to show boys and girls that you must work for success, accept disciplines if you hope for the by-product of happiness, learn tenderness and patience and good manners before you can earn any really satisfying human relationship, if the precepts of the world outside seem to be "as little as possible for as much as possible", or "what is there in this for me?" Worse, the whole clanging and ubiquitous machinery of mass communications in newspaper, film, advertisement and much of broadcasting chants the message of wealth without earning it, success without deserving it, pie in the sky some day soon.'

How true is this, and what are the other accusations one can make against the mass media? They are said to be entertainment to please and distract people, rather than to lead them on to anything better. Dwight MacDonald has written about their impersonality, their lack of standards and total subjection to the spectator.[1] They have a certain area of time and space to fill, and as this expands, with more television channels, more

[1] *Against the American Grain.*

I

newsprint, more teenage money to tap, there is inevitably less talent to go round, and the standard is lowered. It has been said with some truth that the more communications we have, the less is communicated. As the pop market economy depends on a constant turn-over of goods, the emphasis is always on speedy consumption, change and replacement. A mass audience leads the providers to think not of individuals, but of crowds in terms of their lowest common denominator.

This is of course overstated, and the prevailing mood at the conference was not one of condemnation, but more an attitude of cautious discrimination. The mass media can be a positive assistance in education, because of their universality and because the teacher can obviously use them for his own ends. One can quote dreadful examples of the mass media, it is true, but there are also times when they can achieve excellent results. There *is* a lot of bathwater, some of it not very clean, but there is a baby as well. Indeed, a sociologist speaking at the N.U.T. conference made a point in emphasising how *good* he thought the mass media were, given the situation in which they flourished. 'We live in a capitalist commercial society which subsists on profit-making. Newspapers have to survive and they have to get advertisers in order to do this. We also have a grossly uneducated society, which throws boys and girls—8o per cent of our population—out into the world at the age of fifteen,[1] having been taught in large classes by teachers inadequately prepared for their task. These are the facts. You have boys and girls for ten years in all, they leave school at fifteen, and get blind-alley jobs. Given all this, I think it is strange that popular culture is so good rather than that it is so bad.'[2]

But what is the teacher's present attitude towards the mass media? With some exceptions, Jack Longland's complaint still holds true. 'There are almost certainly too many teachers who

---

[1] The figure is now nearer 70 per cent.
[2] Dr A. Tropp, in the National Union of Teachers' *Popular Culture and Personal Responsibility*.

have not got a telly, or if they have, rarely manage to watch it between six and nine when the children mostly do, who practically never visit the cinema, and cannot bear to look at the glossies or the comics; who avoid the more cheese-cakey press. . .and most of them feel that they should not be blamed for these cultural omissions; they have too much to do, and if they had more time they think there are better ways of spending it.. . . Without this knowledge, much of the good they can do will be aborted since the children so clearly are influenced by this other outside world. With it, their teaching becomes stronger and more effective; they can speak to the condition of their boys and girls without the barriers that so often arise in communication through the lack of shared experiences; and they can build on and turn to life-enhancing experience the many good things that can be found among the mass media.'

Time and time again government and independent reports have taken up this theme and urged teachers to spend more time with mass media studies in schools. Of course, some extremely interesting work is being done, but on nothing like the scale desired. This cannot simply be blamed on the pressure of time and exams; in many cases there is a real blockage preventing the teacher from sympathising in any way with I.T.V., modern clothes fashions, pop music and the *Daily Mirror*. Not only does he dislike them himself; so often he condemns them out of hand for his pupils; and those who continue to like them can only be aware of the unbridgeable gap between their teacher's taste and their own.

Undoubtedly one of the reasons for this situation lies in the present social pattern in this country, where sociologists are finding it increasingly easy to define class in terms of cultural as well as economic differences. Thus as incomes tend to level off, class barriers are still maintained by whether you read *The Times*, listen to Shostakovitch, watch *Monitor* and see Ingmar Bergman films, or whether it is the *News of the World*, the top twenty, soap operas and bawdy films.

This picture is of course oversimplified. Some newspapers, notably the *Daily Express*, have an almost equal proportion of readers from every class, while many television programmes and films have a genuinely universal audience. But by and large cultural interests and pursuits do tend to split into middle-class and working-class camps, and the teacher is under an enormous pressure, by forces both outside and inside the school, to maintain 'proper' middle-class standards. These are often characterised by the sort of topics he does *not* talk about, rather than by those that he does discuss. Thus in schools where there is more concern with handing down prescribed cultural standards than with teaching genuine discrimination, such standards can quickly become fused with school authority, so that for the pupils art galleries and Beethoven are seen as 'educational', while 'pops' are the things they can really enjoy after school. No wonder most pupils never read a word of poetry or go to a concert after they have left school.

If the picture is going to change at all, it will mean that the teacher must make some concessions to his pupils' tastes if he is hoping to win genuine sympathy for his own. This means no longer considering culture as a series of algebraic laws (Beethoven = good, pop music = bad), but (as Stuart Hall and A. D. Whannel say) admitting that there is good pop culture as well as bad, just as there is bad posh culture as well as good.[1] Deciding which is which is always very difficult, but we can go a long way by treating each work on its merits, asking the right questions, and listening to what other people have to say. In this way, pupils will be given an *attitude* towards both kinds of culture, rather than ready-made opinions which so often run contrary to their own personal preferences at the time. If we can help a pupil to be articulate and discriminating on what he knows most about, it will be easier for him to discriminate in other fields of culture. A boy who can judge between a good and a bad Western or crime film is on the way to being a good film critic.

[1] *The Popular Arts.*

This should not lead to a ghastly brave new world where Beethoven is considered as good as the latest pop discovery. Direct comparisons do not come into it, since each type of culture normally has a quite different function and fulfils a different need. No-one dances to Beethoven, just as few people listen quietly to the Beatles or any other current pop stars. All I am suggesting is that both can be discussed, and that articulate discussion about one can help with articulate discussion about the other. Discrimination about either culture involves value judgements, which should surely have their place in a school curriculum genuinely concerned with values.

Although no-one would doubt that we should teach cultural discrimination in schools, there may be some who feel we should stop before we get to the mass media, since they are simply not worth the trouble. On cultural grounds alone, history is always proving this point of view to be wrong, and the cultural élite is often a generation late in catching up with aspects of popular culture, such as jazz and the cinema, which have since proved their worth. But there are other reasons why teachers should concern themselves with the mass media. Dr Mark Abrams, talking at the N.U.T. conference, reminded delegates of the enormous hold the mass media have on the lives of young people. 'Today, the average school child aged eight to fifteen spends almost as much time with the mass media as he (and she) spends at school. His weekly diet includes nearly twenty hours watching television, almost two hours of radio listening, the reading of two or three comics, and a visit to the cinema about once a fortnight. For at least half of the older children in this group (i.e. those aged twelve to fifteen) there can be added the reading of one newspaper a day (usually the *Daily Mirror*) and one at the weekend (usually the *Sunday Mirror* or the *News of the World*).'

The same author has calculated elsewhere that the average real weekly wage of teenagers in 1960 was 50 per cent higher than before the war, and that they have a yearly spending power of £900 m., though it should be noticed that his definition of a teenager here covers an age range from thirteen to twenty-five years of age.[1] This is obviously a new situation; never before have teenagers had so much ready money to spend, and the commercial world has not been slow to realise this. Thus the commercial cult of the teenager is born, a strange mixture of reality and artifice, of real wants and created needs. Many older people condemn teenagers for not behaving as they did when they were young, forgetting that the situation has changed and the teenager has the money, time and opportunity as never before to establish himself as a consumer and to demand his own standards. Yet in many ways he is being manipulated, though by commercial rather than conventional forces. Many teenagers may not feel that they want to conform to the commercial image of what a teenager is supposed to like and do, but may feel helpless in the face of so much one-way propaganda. Their parents may also be affected by it. A Slough manufacturer

issued a booklet called 'The Understanding Mother', and subtitled 'How to help your daughter through the sensitive years between the ages of eleven and sixteen'. It gives the following advice: 'The understanding mother knows that her daughter may have an emotional need for a bra even when she is under-developed . . . in order to feel grown up or be like the other girls'. The manufacturer's newspaper advertising makes the following statement: 'Psychological note. She wants to wear a bra and a girdle anyway—whether she really needs it or not. For it is very important for her to be like the other girls—to belong.'[2]

Faced with the many forces which go to make up the teenage cult, and which sometimes preserve their grip right through adulthood, how sad that the school should have so little part in mediating between these pressures and the child itself. One result is that these forces have had their own way, and set their own standards—many of them deplorably low—for far too long.

This book is intended primarily for teachers—whether in school, college, or evening class—who feel they would like to tackle the mass media, but do not know quite where to begin.

[1] *The Teenage Consumer.*
[2] Article by Ray Wills in *Screen Education 5.*

I hope too it will be of general value to other readers interested for their own sake in dissecting and analysing the topics I have discussed. I have tried to give an outline of the different branches of the mass media, covering the issues of content and technique that I think pupils should know about. The mass media are dynamic, and different things become popular every year, but these changes tend to be superficial, and the main framework I have described is unlikely to change very radically. I have also given as many general ideas as I can for practical work in the classroom, in a way which I hope teachers will be able to adapt to their own situations and requirements.

If the teacher still feels he does not know enough of the details of pop culture he should not worry, since his pupils will be pleased to make good the deficiency. His job anyway is to guide discussion rather than lay down the law, and pupils will soon find him out if he insists on 'teaching' pop culture as opposed to talking about it. This is not to say that he should hide or disguise any very strong views he may have on some aspects of 'pop'; his pupils will not mind them so long as he gives them the right to say what they think. Although this sounds a somewhat anarchic situation, it is surprising how soon the teacher and his pupils will find themselves agreeing on general principles, especially if both parties begin the study with as open a mind as possible and make their discoveries together.

Some pupils, but only a very few, accept branches of the mass media uncritically and *in toto*. For them it is an escape to a land of milk and honey, or as one pupil once said, mink and money, where problems are solved as soon as they have been stated, and whose only relationship to the real world is that it has *no* relationship. For such pupils the mass media obviously provide something that is grossly deficient in their actual life, and as Marx would say, have replaced religion as 'the opium of the people'. But most pupils have a far tougher attitude towards them: they like what they think is good, and, when they remember, are critical of the bad. Surrounded by an entertainment world that throws all it has in the direction of the teenager in the way of mass persuasion, since it is this group that spends most money on it, is it surprising that this critical sense often becomes dulled? The teacher will find, however, that it is nearly always there, though to begin with it is hesitant and inarticulate.

Literacy is not a single skill, something achieved once for all with the power to translate written symbols into sounds. It involves the power to invest words with meaning, to recognise the ideas which somebody else wishes to convey and to use them oneself to express the thoughts which without their help would remain fleeting and inchoate. 'How do I know what I want to say until I've said it?' is a childish but not a foolish, remark.[1]

Often, when they are faced with pop culture, pupils will accept the bad for want of anything better. They are usually not helped in this difficulty, but actively misled. Apart from a few Knoxian blasts from pulpit and rostrum, most voices that can be heard talking about the mass media do so with a note of hysterical lyricism: films are the 'greatest', singers are the 'mostest', advertised products are always 'unique', and so on down the whole range of over-heated hyperbole. The teacher is in an ideal position to supply a third voice, that neither accepts nor rejects the mass media on principle, but dissects, analyses and appraises. His material is at hand wherever he looks, and he will find such lessons a stimulating experience both for himself and for the class. Pupils nearly always react with enthusiasm, and later with knowledge and judgement; it is as if they have been waiting to talk about these things for some time.

[1]Ministry of Education, *Half Our Future.*

CHAPTER I

THE PRESS

The average pupil now at school will, as an adult, read at least one paper a day and two on Sundays. Some may conclude from this that young people will be seeing quite enough of newspapers when they leave school, and that for the present it would be better to concentrate on more rewarding topics. I do not share this view. If the press is still to be a genuine fourth estate it needs *informed* readers to complete the partnership. A pupil may later become an avid newspaper reader but may read only the sports page or the chatty domestic columns. Refugees arriving in England before the last war were often appalled at the ignorance they found about world affairs; and from the results of spot checks carried out more recently on simple questions like the name of the prime minister and the leader of the opposition, it appears that some of this ignorance is still with us. This lack of knowledge is often blamed on the press, but this is clearly unfair; every paper prints news on topics like foreign affairs, even though some editors may be quite certain that most of their readers will ignore it. Yet on the other hand, if a reader of certain newspapers does get as far as the less 'popular' news he may be only slightly better off, since he may not know that on occasions he is reading a highly biased or quite inaccurate report.

A study of newspapers therefore has many different functions. It can help pupils find their way round the wide variety of topics covered in a newspaper and can also show them, by the comparison of different reports of the same news, that there are many roads to the truth—or away from it! In this way pupils will be introduced to newspapers they would never ordinarily dream of consulting and to news topics which they have previously ignored, and learn both about what is happening in the world and the different ways in which this might be conveyed. In case this sounds like a solemn exercise in applied civics, it should be pointed out that pupils always enjoy these lessons, some never quite getting over the excitement and incongruity of reading a real newspaper in class! From the teacher's point of view papers are also extremely convenient to work with since they are cheap, highly topical, and have almost endless possibilities for work with a wide variety of pupils.

When planning these lessons the teacher will find that books he might consult about the press generally fall into two quite irreconcilable categories. For some critics, the press has never been the same since Lord Northcliffe brought in the tabloid newspaper with its sensationalist headlines, which in itself is seen as a sort of fall from grace. Thus all popular papers are also the 'gutter' press or examples of 'yellow' journalism, and we hear harrowing stories of misrepresentation, exaggeration, lying, bribery, unwelcome intrusion and biased selection and suppression of news based largely on the whims of the paper's chief advertisers. Such critics are often excellent on the need for constant vigilance on the part of the reader, and it is owing to this sort of informed criticism that we now have the Press Council. Yet too much of this spirit can lead to an arid 'You can't believe anything you read in the papers' sort of attitude, and rather than helping readers to pick out what is good in popular papers, tends to dismiss the whole genre out of hand with the implicit assumption that we should all read the same few quality newspapers (which, incidentally, often miss their fair share of necessary criticism in this sort of study).

On the other hand, there are more chatty books, written usually by ex-journalists, which generally specialise in technical information and loving descriptions of the layout and daily routine of a newspaper office, but also have their share of stories, this time about brilliant scoops, reporters who faced death in order to get some news, and editors who transformed a dull rag into a dazzlingly entertaining newspaper read by millions. If there is any reference in these books to questionable ethics in some news reporting it may be brushed aside with slogans in the spirit of 'Better read than dead'. Once more, it is valuable for a class to hear of some of the real difficulties under which a journalist has to work, and why some of his reports are not as accurate as they might be. But this sort of viewpoint is often quite uncritical and will not help a pupil to see why the press is ever criticised, let alone what the criticism is usually about.

Both these positions of course are taken up with very much more subtlety than I have indicated here, and a book like *Dangerous Estate*[1] manages to cover both aspects; but in general the teacher is left with alternatives neither of which is particularly helpful. If he is going to teach that all papers that write in a style different from that used in the quality press are morally evil he will not make much impression; if on the other hand he is merely going to show pupils how technically brilliant and entertaining each paper is in its different way, he might really save himself the trouble and try something else. In fact the teacher can take a third path: by accepting each paper for what it is, and helping his pupils to see the main differences between them all. Any criticisms of individual papers that come out of this will be based not on prejudice but on the performance of each paper when compared with its rivals.

The teacher should always be a participant in these lessons, not an onlooker. The class itself may be far better equipped to assess how adequately the newspaper is dealing with sport, show-business, pop music, teenage fashion and motoring news, and in these cases the teacher might learn something himself. He will of course have his own taste in newspapers, but in this case he must avoid being too censorious about others' judgement, since mass-circulation newspapers belong to the home, not the school, and the teacher must tread delicately so as not to offend home loyalties too brutally. Before going on to make a content analysis however, pupils should understand something about the newspaper industry at the moment; this they can do

[1] Francis Williams.

by listening to the teacher and by following up what he says by looking at the papers themselves.

HOW A NEWSPAPER GETS ITS NEWS

A big daily will have from fifty to one hundred full-time reporters, most of them centred on London, but some stationed in provincial cities. The class might like to collect as many of their names as possible, and to collate them with the jobs they do. We can then discover how specialised are the services a newspaper offers us. For example, how many papers have a regular medical, scientific, educational and air correspondent? Which papers keep regular correspondents abroad, and in how many countries? It is both revealing and relevant to our assessment of them to see what specialised functions some papers do or do not cater for. Staff reporters often have to travel, and if one is sent somewhere, he is acknowledged as 'Our Special Correspondent'. If he is not a journalist, but regularly sends news to the paper, he may be called just 'Our Correspondent' (there may be up to 1,500 of these people, known in the profession as 'stringers'). Lastly, someone who contributes news but who has no previous connections with the paper is merely 'A Correspondent'. These services are helped out by huge news agencies, which have their own reporters and are liberally used by all newspapers. Of these, the Press Association and Exchange Telegraph deal with home news, while Reuters, British United Press and Associated Press deal with foreign news.

These agencies are usually—but not always—acknowledged by the papers that use them. Each paper will treat the agency material in a different way: it will be paraphrased, cut, added to and even slipped into a column attributed to 'Our Special Correspondent'. The ways in which different papers use the same material is often very revealing, and the class will enjoy piecing the evidence together if this is possible. Finally, when the class wants to decide which paper during the week gives the most accurate report on some trouble spot or important political event overseas, it can use *Keesing's Contemporary Archives* as a yardstick. This is a weekly bulletin, to be found in most reference libraries, which gives a purely factual account of the week's political, economic and social events throughout the world. It is not very interesting reading, but its monumental accuracy and thoroughness will tell us whether some papers are consistently misreporting or omitting facts about foreign news.

Reporters usually have to work in a hurry, and some inaccuracy is inevitable. When an American team climbed Everest, practically no paper could agree how high the mountain was, while the cost of the trip varied from £116,000 in the *Daily Express* to £200,000 in the *Daily Sketch*. All quantitative news published in newspapers is liable to some inaccuracy if it has been taken down in a hurry, and no pupil should feel that he has 'finally nailed Fleet Street' when he discovers an error of this sort. On other occasions, however, the fluctuations may be so extreme that one begins to suspect the newspaper of bias: estimated numbers at political meetings or on the Aldermaston March tend to relate directly to the paper's attitude towards these events.

Although he is in a hurry, the good journalist must make sure that his sources of information are reliable. Sometimes he may have no sources at all, and must of necessity base his report on hints and guesses. This happens when a well-publicised confidential meeting breaks up without issuing a press statement; but some journalists ask for trouble by presenting the supposed conversations at these meetings so confidently that one feels they must either have been under the table or at least at the keyhole. It is obviously wiser for a journalist who does not have all the facts to admit it; and hints and guesses should be given for what they are worth.

The *Report of the Tribunal Appointed to Inquire into the Vassall Case and Related Matters* is a mine of information on these points. It will be remembered that it was suggested after the trial and imprisonment of Vassall, an Admiralty clerk, for espionage, that the security services, his seniors and even the government had been negligent in not discovering his activities earlier. Articles published in the press at the time came in for a full examination at the tribunal, and many of them emerged with little credit. Thus a journalist on the *Sunday Telegraph* wrote: 'John Vassall, the convicted Admiralty spy, was known to British diplomats in Moscow as a homosexual. But, according to Foreign Office circles, reports on him by the Embassy were ignored by the Admiralty'. When questioned, the journalist admitted that his remark was not based on any contact that he had himself with any member of the Foreign Office, though he thought that he was reflecting broadly the opinions that he believed to be held in the Foreign Office. Pupils should learn the difference between an 'official' source and a 'reliable' one, which can prove most unreliable indeed.

Even the possession of a source is not the end of a journalist's worries, since the source itself might be wrong. He may, of course, encourage this by putting too much pressure on his witness. The statement of two cleaners about Vassall played an important part in the newspaper campaign against the government of the time. When questioned, one of them admitted making a statement which was frankly misleading, while the other denied having said most of the things the paper had printed. The Report noted that one of these witnesses had spent up to sixteen hours with the journalist, who had also paid her a large sum of money; not a situation conducive to disinterested retrospection. In a case like this, where there is little information, rumour and gossip spiral to an alarming height. In such situations the official world must to some extent share the blame if it does not take the press more into its confidence. In their desperate search for 'hard' news, many of the newspaper stories in the Vassall case were based on stories in other papers, which in turn were either inaccurate or grossly exaggerated.

Even if the facts given by the source are strictly true, the journalist must make sure that there is no ambiguity lurking in them which might lead him and his readers into pitfalls. On

4 November 1962 *The People* printed these 'facts' about Vassall:

Vassall's neighbour in 1954 and 1955 was Mr Stanley Johnson, formerly correspondent in Moscow for the American press. . . . Said Mr Johnson, 'I saw him almost every day during 1954. More than once I saw his face covered in cream'. . . . He stated nobody could make any mistake about Vassall. He shared his flat with two other British Embassy clerks, but they would have nothing to do with him. They used the two bedrooms in the flat and made him sleep on the sofa in the living room.

At the tribunal the facts emerged as these: the cream was Nivea cream, used by many people as a protection against the cold, and the sleeping arrangements lasted a few weeks only, after Vassall's first arrival in Moscow, where he lived temporarily in a flat already occupied by two others. He then moved into a two-bedroom flat with a friend who never even suspected that Vassall was homosexual. Such is the danger of generalisation; and such are the difficulties facing journalists with their editor's deadline rapidly approaching, and no hard news in sight. It is a situation which may bring out the best or occasionally the worst in someone. We should not excuse journalists who burst in on tragic domestic situations or come to highly irresponsible deductions in search of hot news, but at least we should understand the situation which produces these results.

CRITICISMS THAT CAN BE LEVELLED AT NEWSPAPERS

The annual report of the Press Council is invaluable to the teacher, since it deals with the hard core of complaints made about the press each year. He should read to his class some of the examples quoted in it, and these can be discussed before he tells them of the Council's actual decision. It is interesting to see which newspapers have most complaints made about them, and which of them are most often censured by the Council. Of course, there is no reason why pupils themselves should not make use of the Press Council, should they come across something they feel very strongly about. The Council is an important body with a skilled staff, and pupils should obviously not be encouraged to send in flippant complaints; but it is an excellent idea for them to know that they can write to the Council, since its whole machinery depends on regular contact with the public, most of whom neither know nor care about this privilege.

We have already dealt with criticisms of inaccuracies and unjustified deductions. Bias in reporting is another frequent complaint. American journalists are always amazed at the amount of 'editorialising' they find in our papers, where a reporter brings in his own subjective viewpoint into what looks like a straightforward record of the facts. American papers are supposed to have a tradition of reporting the news without comment, but according to A. J. Liebling, the position is not so different from our own. He describes how the right-wing American press treats labour disputes in different sections of the community; the parallel cases he chooses involved the meat producers, who were forcing up meat prices by withholding their goods from the market, and the coal miners, who were withholding their labour to force up their wages. Of the press treatment, Liebling writes, 'There was a note of understanding approval—even I may say of affection—in most of the stories about the cattlemen, who were represented as rugged, wholesome, humorous individual enterprisers. . . .Maybe it's my imagination, but the papers seem to me to be taking a bleaker view of the coal miners, who are using exactly the same tactics'. This he describes later as the doctrine of 'unilateral original sin in labour disputes'.[1] Pupils can still find this in descriptions of strikes in our own right-wing press, just as they will find that on the extreme left-wing it is the management that can do no good. It is sad that so often neither type of paper will give us the actual facts of the dispute. What is the wage the employers are offering? What are the strikers demanding, and what are the wages in comparable sectors of the economy?

Pupils are always interested by bias in reporting, perhaps because it makes adults seem to behave like children. They can

[1] *The Press.*

become adept at recognising it, and can talk for some time on the more subtle implications of quite small examples, such as:

'Sir Basil gave no figures for the number of B.O.A.C. workers who will be redundant' (*Daily Herald*).

'State-owned B.O.A.C. . . . admitted . . . some staff will have to be axed. About 1,000, it is believed, will have to go' (*Daily Express*).

The *Report of the Royal Commission on the Press* (1949) stated that 'In reporting election meetings it was general for each newspaper to suggest that the speakers belonging to the party which it supported were received either in awed silence or with thunderous cheers, whereas the opposing speakers were constantly heckled and booed'. Does this still apply to reports of election and parliamentary proceedings?

Another very frequent charge against the press is that of sensationalism. A common technique is for a paper to deny in large print a rumour that few people will even have heard of—up to that moment. Such newspapers often trick their audience into reading a column by heading it with an exciting but quite misleading caption, or by singling out for the introductory sentence (the 'intro') some personal story which is quite unrepresentative of the actual news report itself. Another popular practice is to begin the report with a provocative question, and to keep the answer, which is usually a lame one, until the end. All these devices disguise a really unimportant piece of news, which we would normally not bother to read. Much that is printed in the press is appallingly trivial; the teacher can discuss this with pupils, and see whether he and they can agree on the nature of this triviality. It is noticeable that when sensationalist papers really do get hold of a dramatic piece of news they often manage to kill its real interest by smothering it with over-heated adjectives.

Some newspapers also play on their readers' interest in sex. Hardly any piece of news is too irrelevant to accompany the photograph of a semi-nude girl, while turgid court reports of sexual assaults make up the staple diet of at least one popular national newspaper. With the help of a shocked and sententious style, such stories can pass themselves off in readers' minds as records of moral disapproval and legal punishment, but not before all conceivable and printable details of the crimes committed have been fully savoured.

The ethics of reporting essentially private affairs could also be discussed. Several countries have attempted to lay down a code of behaviour on this matter; in Sweden a journalist is asked to agree that 'Publicity that violates the sanctity of privacy must be avoided, unless it is imperatively in the public interest', while the American society of newspaper editors puts it more succinctly: 'Public right must be served, not public curiosity'. Our own National Union of Journalists has stated that 'in obtaining news or pictures, reporters should do nothing that could cause pain or humiliation to innocent, bereaved, or otherwise distressed persons'. These codes are often ignored in the countries where they have been agreed upon, and the class should certainly look out for any further breaches. It is certainly made very difficult where the victim is a willing participant. One paper printed the story of a six-year-old girl who was due to die of a blood disease before she reached her teens. The paper was criticised for publishing something which was bound to have bad effects on an already sad situation, but it defended itself by pointing out that the mother had not only agreed to this story but had also posed for the photograph with the child.

'Cheque-book journalism'—the buying of exclusive stories, especially confessions of notorious people—is another problem that no code of conduct has ever successfully covered, since these stories, although condemned by most critics, go down very well with the public. No-one would wish to withhold facts, but whether this justifies paying a call-girl or murderer up to £23,000 for their memoirs is another matter. There is even less reason to take these stories seriously when they finally appear, since they are nearly always 'ghosted' by the paper's staff writers, and with their ready-made journalistic clichés lack even the ring of truth. So long as we have freedom of the press, such stories are bound to appear, though the class can discuss whether they do the reputation of the press any good. Only recently a notorious 'model' was able to boast that she was under contract to half Fleet Street.

Gossip columnists, who were once frequently criticised, are not now as powerful as they once were, but they are still worth a careful inspection. The circles they move in are still those quite inaccessible to nearly all the papers' readers, and the clothes, jewels and food described are similarly out of reach. At best these columnists can be witty and informative; otherwise they still seem to cater for malice, envy, curiosity and class consciousness. Their columns provide interesting material for study.

HOW NEWS IS PRESENTED

The way and position in which the newspaper actually prints its news can give us a fair idea of the importance its sub-editor thinks each item has, and makes for interesting comparisons between different papers. The main physical variables to look out for are the amount of space given to a story, its position in the paper and on the page, and the size and character of its headings and type. Stories that editors think will interest their readers will obviously be given ample space and prominent headings, and they will be positioned probably 'above the fold' and on the right hand side, since this is the part of the paper most people look at first (this does not hold true of the front page, where by tradition the main story is placed on the left of the page). The least popular part of a paper is on the bottom left hand side, and it is interesting to see which items find their way there. As well as its position, we must also notice whether the news surrounding our story colours the way in which we read it. A story printed on the front page, surrounded by other important items, looks different when reproduced, say, on the woman's page. When we see sports news printed on the front page, we know something extraordinary has happened.

We should also observe how many different kinds of type the printer uses, and in what ways, if any, they also colour our reaction to the story.

In the actual writing of the news, we can assess by comparison with other papers what points the journalist emphasises, and which he omits altogether. Do these omissions materially alter the report, or are they merely for the sake of brevity? Journalists have also been known to quote remarks and facts out of context; an inspection of some West End theatre hoardings and a comparison later with what was actually written in the drama review will soon show London pupils how quoting out of context can transform any piece of prose ever written, and, in these cases, occasionally change a hostile review into a favourable one.

Much of one's reaction to a piece of news depends upon the style in which it is presented. Before he begins to analyse the different methods of writing-up a story, the pupil must have some understanding of the emotive uses to which language can be put. He must appreciate that there are word-couples, like 'thin' and 'slim', and 'extravagant' and 'generous' which describe the same sort of thing but have different tones of voice associated with them. This point is so important that it is worth doing an exercise where all the complimentary words are changed to pejorative ones without otherwise changing the objective meaning of the piece concerned. Thus a friendly report of a politician might describe him as 'intelligent, confident, with an exuberant manner and a healthy will to win'. A hostile account may paraphrase this as 'sharp, vain, immature and a bad loser'. Professor R. Quirk gives an example of an even more loaded viewpoint. One imaginary account describes 'an elderly gentleman . . . reading his Sunday paper in the park . . . when a dog jumped upon him and upset him so that he was forced to kick at the animal'. The second account describes 'a lively puppy that playfully accosted a man who promptly stamped on it, showing no feeling for our dumb friends'.[1]

[1] *The Use of English* (Longmans).

There are many other tricks of style that help to colour the news as we read it. On the one hand we can find the pompous style, with words that create a spurious impression of profundity, and on the other we have the very basic 'sledge-hammer' style of the tabloids, which seems to give an impression of really frank open-handed discussion, but might also be dealing in dangerous over-simplifications. There is also the hysterical style, found in some sports columns, which pupils greatly enjoy paraphrasing into more sober English, and the cliché-ridden style, with its cosy but jaded appeal. Sir Linton Andrews, former chairman of the Press Council, writes that the worst sort of cliché is the one enclosed in inverted commas, such as 'a shot in the dark'. He also mentions mechanical joinings, like 'hasty retreat' or 'canny Scot'.[1] Too much of this sort of thing has a serious effect: as Somerset Maugham points out, 'The press, in fact, kills the individuality of those who write for it. People who write for the press seem to lose the faculty of seeing things for themselves; they see from a generalised standpoint, vividly often, sometimes with hectic brightness, yet never with . . . idiosyncracy'.[2] It is noticeable that the style of a particular newspaper often engulfs that of its writers, until they all sound exactly the same. It is interesting for older pupils to try to discover what this style consists of, and which journalists working for the paper are able to manage without it. An all-inclusive style is not only to be found in the popular dailies; one remembers the run currently popular terms have had in the quality press, like 'Angry Young Man', or words like 'sick' and 'cool', or 'wry' and 'taut', which eventually lose their meaning.

Another popular style, which often covers a basic lack of anything really worth saying, is the cosy 'you and me' style of the columnist who addresses each reader as if they were on intimate terms, and radiates what Richard Hoggart described as a 'phoney sense of belongingness'. This approach, which is designed to make the reader forget that there may be twelve

[1] *Problems of an Editor.*
[2] *The Summing Up* (Heinemann).

million other people who read that columnist too, is not peculiar to journalism, and often occurs in mass media which feel they must compensate for their distance from their audience by the increased intimacy of their approach. The confidential tones of the popular columnist, the stereotyped fan letter from the pop singer, and the 'sincere' smile of the television personality all have the same thing in common: a fantastic game with numbers, where a mass audience is manipulated to feel that each member of it is a personal friend. In many cases the audience responds by sending back sometimes pathetic letters and presents. It seems wrong that emotion should be stirred up and squandered in this way. There must be better uses for it, and perhaps the teacher can suggest some.

CLASSWORK ON THE PRESS

When pupils are doing a project on newspapers, the most useful way for them to assemble the material is to paste newspaper cuttings on to separate sheets of punched paper, since, left unsupported, the cuttings deteriorate quickly. They can then easily be preserved in a folder. Each cutting should be headed with the name of the newspaper, its date, and any other explanation or comment, which will of course vary with the particular assignment. These comments can be scattered throughout the work; or the pupil can assemble his evidence, and then write a short essay, using the cuttings as he wishes. If the project involves following one story through different newspapers, the teacher must make sure that he has enough newspapers and copies to make the study possible. Every pupil can normally be expected to bring at least one paper to school for the lesson, but the teacher must make sure that he does not get ten copies of the *Daily Express* and no *Times* or *Daily Worker*. Although no-one would discourage pupils from choosing projects they are naturally in sympathy with, their assignments should be as varied as possible, and the cricket enthusiast should only be allowed to get away with one cricket story. There are plenty of interesting topics to choose from, without saddling the pupil with something he hates. The teacher should always discuss with the class what he wants it to do, and everybody should pool ideas on how to do it. In the front of his folder each pupil should keep a list of all the available national papers, so that in a comparative study he can tick off each one as he comes to it and not miss any. This is also a convenient device for making sure that pupils consult papers they would normally never dream of reading.

Before he gets on to comparative studies, it is useful for a pupil to be able to find his way around one newspaper, and to be able to recognise the different types of news and features. He will also find it interesting to see how much space his favourite newspaper gives to various items, and how it compares with other newspapers, which can be analysed by other members of the class. The results can be written into one enormous comparative chart, and they always create interest. If this is thought to be too elaborate, a few selected categories can be chosen for comparison. Thus one chart might compare the price, total amount of space available, advertising rates,[1] circulation[2] and the amount of home and foreign political news. Another might cover the arts, sports, gossip columns and advertisements. The variations for comparison are endless, and certainly enough to give a class plenty to do. One can soon see the different pattern of priorities which each paper has; but analysis can also go much deeper than this.

The intelligent pupil can go on from here to discover the rough outline of the paper's readership, and its likes and dislikes. He can get some idea of its social background from the figures quoted in Appendix B, and he can add to this by noting what sort of jobs and goods are advertised in the particular newspaper, and to what sort of people they would appeal. There may be some clues he can use, like the presence of a city page, or extensive coverage of greyhound racing. The

[1] See Appendix A.
[2] See Appendix B.

tone and content of the advertisements for the newspaper will also help. This is not to suggest that, once a pupil has found out that a newspaper caters particularly for his sort of social class, he should use this as grounds for choosing it. On the contrary, suppositions on a newspaper's part on what is good for its special readership are often extremely limiting both for the paper and for its readers. The pupil has a right, however, to know what the readership of a paper is, and to discover from this in what way the paper chooses to cater for the supposed tastes of this readership. After this, he can draw his own conclusions.

For this analysis, pupils will need rulers and rough paper for doing sums, and should work out the amount of space given to each subject in terms of column inches, so that the ruler need only be used vertically. Those who are good at maths can later work out what the result is in terms of percentage of the whole. Categories of news and features which I have found useful for a breakdown of this sort are:

1. Advertisements, classified and display.
2. Cartoons
    (a) Political
    (b) Humorous
    (c) Strip serials.
3. Sports news.
4. Photographs and captions.
5. Crime, legal and accident news.
6. Foreign and political news.
7. Home political news.
8. Leading articles.
9. Personality and social gossip.
10. The arts.
11. Readers' letters.
12. Financial, economic and industrial news.
13. Women's news.
14. Domestic news.

15. Foreign news.
16. Features.
17. Horoscope.
18. Scientific and technical news.
19. Children's features.
20. 'Human interest' stories.
21. Miscellaneous (radio, weather, gardening, puzzles, competitions, etc.).

Many of these distinctions will be difficult for the class to appreciate, and the teacher could well begin the study by spending some time defining each category and asking the class to find examples of each. In this way he will be performing a useful comprehension exercise, and will also be directing the class's attention towards news it might not have understood or even known about before. A useful reference for this exercise can be found on page 242 of the *Report of the Royal Commission on the Press* (1949), which lists all conceivable categories of news and their subdivision in great detail. For quick decisions on whether a particular piece of news belongs, say, in the domestic or economic category, this can be an extremely useful yardstick, and prevents the teacher making a different decision when he is next asked a similar question.

Some pupils might be interested to compare the different editions of one paper published on the same day. This can be done with evening papers, or else they can write to the circulation manager of a large London daily enclosing enough money to buy about half a dozen of the different editions which are printed from very early in the morning onwards. Pupils should notice news items which have replaced previous ones. What has prompted the editor to make this change? If the new edition contains a précis of a previous item, what points have been omitted? Does the new edition ever correct a mistake in the old one? Do some of the news photographs change and get better in later editions? Is there any evidence of hurry in some of the early stories? In this way pupils can get something of the atmosphere of a large newsroom, and the constant arrival of new items that have to be included.

Detailed comparison between two or more newspapers

A good start for this sort of exercise is simply to take the headlines of different newspapers on the same day and compare them. When this is done over a number of days, quite a good picture of each paper emerges, and the results look impressive on display. It has been neatly done by Raymond Williams, where he compares the headlines of the English dailies over one week.[1] The characters of the different papers are soon made obvious not only in the nature of the story they choose, but in the words they use to describe it. Thus *The Times* will lead with 'Cheering crowds hail Major Gagarin', which appears in the *Daily Sketch* as 'Ga-Ga over Gaga'. Another day *The Times* leads with 'U.S. missile detector launched' while the *Daily Sketch* gives its headline, with, as Sir Linton Andrews would say, the utmost typographical emphasis, as 'One ton whale amok at Kew'. Other papers tend to fluctuate between these two poles, both in vocabulary and subject matter. Sometimes the differences are small, but still interesting:

'B.O.A.C. to cut fleet and staff. Increasing competition from former colonies' (*The Times*).

'B.O.A.C. to cut its staff and fleet. New competition from the Commonwealth' (*The Guardian*).

Apart from their comparative interest, headlines put together give an excellent quick survey of the week's news, in all its aspects. In their urge to abbreviate and sometimes sensationalise, headlines often make weird reading. Professor Quirk gives some choice examples of this.[2] 'MacArthur flies back to front.' 'Liverpool tea breaks leader under fire.' 'Virgin lands job for disgraced Red.' The American Society of Newspaper Editors have declared that 'headlines should be fully warranted by the

---

[1] *Communications.*
[2] *The Use of English.*

contents of the articles which they surmount'. Is this always so? Before long, the class should find many examples of exaggeration, omission, and even plain misstatement. The Royal Commission on the Press (1949) mentioned a *Daily Worker* headline which read 'Bevin to U.S. "Your Humble Servant" ', when these words were never said on that or any other occasion. The class should also look at the smaller headings in each paper, to see how the same item of news can be presented in many different ways.

Then the pupil can compare ordinary news stories; film, theatre, book, television and fashion reviews; games reports; political cartoons and photographs of the same subject. He can also compare the topics of the readers' correspondence in the different papers. Each pupil can take charge of a particular item and prepare a report on the differences of presentation, factual content and interpretation that he can find.

It is good for him to see that there are two points of view. If he reads 'I have seen most of Graveney's vintage innings, but few have matched this one in terms of quality and timing' in the *Daily Mail*, and 'It was not Tom at his masterful best' in the *Daily Mirror*, perhaps it will make him realise that he should accept other people's opinions with caution, and should make up his own mind whenever possible. Film and book reviews give the pupil a better chance to measure his own sensibilities against those of the critic employed by the paper he reads. Of a period film, the critic in the *Daily Telegraph* said that there were 'many incidental absurdities in the semi-scanning dialogue', while the *Daily Mirror* found that 'the dialogue rarely falls into the idiocies so often found in this type of costume epic'. The pupil can decide for himself when he sees the film.

As well as discovering differences of opinion or straightforward bias, he will sometimes find that someone has blundered. 'Not the least remarkable aspect of all this is that Pataudi cannot see properly through his left eye which was injured in a motor accident two years ago'; 'Pataudi tells me that operations on his right eye . . . have failed to restore its sight and have been abandoned' (two quotations from the same issue of the *Sunday Telegraph*).

Hard-boiled journalists can even be coy at times. 'Cowdrey, well-bolstered fore and aft, retracted his bottom to avoid contact. Instead his leg stump was flattened behind him' (*The Observer*). This part of Cowdrey was also roundly described as his 'ample buttocks' by the *Sunday Times*. Euphemisms crept in with the *Sunday Telegraph*'s 'not unsubstantial stern' and the *Sunday Citizen*'s 'considerable posterior'. But the paper that prides itself most on its outspokenness, the *Sunday Mirror*, could manage nothing better than 'rear portion'.

Every day a newspaper makes predictions, from weather reports and racing—too trivial to spend any time on—to by-elections and budget allocations. Interesting prophecies of this sort should be stored up by pupils in their folders, with a blank space underneath for following them up. It is interesting to see which papers prophesy most accurately: not always the ones the teacher expects. 'What the stars foretell' is another form of prophecy, patronised by several papers. Very often, because the language is kept deliberately vague, these predictions are fairly safe. It is difficult to go wrong with easy predictions like a journey in August or a pleasant social evening around 25 December. But it should not be too long before a pupil discovers a complete contradiction between two papers' horoscopes, which is instructive for those pupils and their parents who take such things semi-seriously. What would they do if born under Pisces, and advised by the *Daily Mirror* that 'You will tend to feel irritable and confused and slightly depressed', but reassured by the *Daily Mail* on the same day that 'People enjoy your company. A good time to visit old friends'. If born under Leo they are in for a confusing time during the summer sales, since the *Sunday Mirror* warns them 'Don't be swept up into some indiscreet move that could place a monetary strain on family affairs', but the *News of the World* insists that they should 'Go after the things you want. This is no time for standing still'. Horoscopes also portray the occasional class leaning: 'Trouble with servants this week' (*Queen*). Political cartoons make very good comparative material. What is the subject they are dealing with, and what point of view does the cartoonist take? A pupil can cut out different cartoonists' versions of a current political figure, stick them side by side in his folder, and write about each paper's image of the same person. Another pupil can keep a daily record of one paper's political cartoons, and, by adding a few explanatory notes under each drawing, can keep a useful and easy-to-read political diary.

Pupils should also compare photographs of the same incidents or personalities in different newspapers. Which papers have the best cameramen? Does one picture emphasise details omitted or underplayed in another newspaper? How often is the same picture from a free-lance photographer reproduced in more than one paper? Are the pictures ever obviously retouched? Do pictures of political figures appear the same in different papers, or does one paper always print unflattering reproductions, in key with the political cartoons appearing in that paper? Occasionally newspapers publish photographs which have no news value but are there solely for their striking appearance, and pupils might like to collect some of these for their folders.

The class should also examine some of the myths about journalists, made popular by some American films. How often is the journalist really on the spot? Recently some of them were reporting events in Tibet from a vantage point some three hundred miles away. If there is any doubt of a journalist's exact position in respect to the actual event, an atlas should be consulted. Does a paper ever really get a 'scoop' these days, or have modern communications put a stop to this? It is interesting to examine items that appear in only one paper; how often are they a scoop, and how often are they merely bits of news not important enough to be printed elsewhere? Which paper gets the most scoops?

More advanced work can be done with legal or political

reports, often reported closely in the more expensive papers. With the raw material at his disposal, a pupil can look over the shoulder of a journalist of another paper, and watch him select, omit, and occasionally distort. An exhaustive (and exhausting) way to do this more thoroughly is to get hold of a report in Hansard and to analyse it into main headings and subheadings, in the manner of a brief précis. These should then be arranged into a column, beginning with the first point and ending with the last. Then the pupil can check each item with each newspaper report, a 1/ by the side of a heading will show that the paper reported it, while a ½/ will indicate a generalised reference. In this way the pupil will really understand how the selection of facts as well as their interpretation can explain the bias of a particular newspaper report. A full version of this technique can be found on page 270 of the *Report of the Royal Commission on the Press* (1949). From it, pupils can also get some idea of how successfully a paper is able to reproduce complex issues and arguments into readable form without obscuring or simplifying essential points.

Other exercises

If it is already there, the newspaper can be brought into more formal English periods. Pupils can follow a correspondence right through, collect all the cuttings, and comment on each of the letters, perhaps writing one themselves. An editorial is a good way of beginning a discussion, and it is also a useful model for a short essay. Television and film reviews, together with advertisements, are essential for work described later in this book.

Non-political cartoons can also be used by the class, perhaps for a more light-hearted project. What sort of people appear in them, and what are their habits? Colin MacInnes does this very engagingly when he writes about the three *Daily Express* families: the Giles, Appleby and Lancaster groups. Acting on hints from the drawings, MacInnes describes each character in the cartoons. Of the father in Giles' family, he writes, 'He must be at least in his sixties, since it appears he served in World War I as well as 2. His dress and habits are resolutely proletarian (shirt-sleeves indoors, pints of truant wallop with the lads, bawdy flirtations and fundamental loyalty to the home), and in character he is entirely insensitive and endlessly patient, though liable to outbursts of exasperated rage.'[1] MacInnes also notes the odd stereotyped characters who crop up in Giles from a world that is only half real: colonial governors decked with plumage, baby-kissing politicians, bespatted and tea-drinking bureaucrats, and monotonously ridiculous foreigners. Andy Capp in the *Daily Mirror* is another portentous figure for analysis. Is he really a figure from the modern world?

Most cartoons, however, do not run in families, and they too often refer to curiously inbred situations which exist far more in the cartoonist's mind than in real life. We all know how a typical cartoon character spends a normal working day. He is difficult to wake up, and needs a blistering remark from his wife to get him awake. At breakfast he reads a newspaper that totally hides his face. He is late for the office, and has to face his boss who is meaningfully looking at the clock, which is permanently set at something like ten past nine. At work, he will either chase his secretary round the desk, or she will sit demurely on his lap only to be surprised by his wife on an unexpected visit. On his way home, he is taken out by some friends and becomes very drunk. The day ends with his arrival home, trilby hat crushed, hanging on to the door handle with a bemused smile. Almost always his wife will be sitting under the clock, with a rolling pin in her hand. There are many other aspects of his life the class can write about: his weekends, holidays and childhood. Why do these themes keep cropping up?

Serial strip cartoons, some of which can be witty and delightfully imagined, can be used by the teacher as a help towards narrative writing. One of the best of these, 'Flook' in the *Daily Mail*, has had some adventures written by Sir Compton Mackenzie, who took over the story for a time from the original

---

[1] *England, Half English.*

31

author and artist, Wally Fawkes. Pupils can be given a series of 'frames' and asked to transcribe them into their own narrative. This means that a pupil must keep the dialogue, but will use his own words to describe who says it, in what manner, when and why. This is not a creative approach, but it can be useful for backward pupils who have difficulty in covering more than half a page with their own writing.

Perhaps late in the summer term the form can try to produce its own newspaper, using the national dailies as a very rough model. There are enough jobs in this to occupy everyone in a large form. All the different newspaper jobs already mentioned can be adapted for school use; other popular features include: opinion polls, puzzles and queries, crosswords, profiles of school characters, do-it-yourself advice, nature and gardening, poems, short stories, drawings and the inevitable strip cartoon. Advertisements for school dinners and forthcoming events can be useful as well as amusing. If the whole thing is too unwieldy to gather together into one edition, it should be pinned, preferably on typed sheets, round the wall. However limited its circulation, the class will still enjoy writing it.

Newspapers and slow readers

Every teacher who takes a remedial form knows how difficult it is to find reading material. Boys and girls approaching school-leaving age but retaining a reading age of below ten seem an insuperable problem, since most of the books that would suit their reading ability are far too infantile in tone. A similar problem is presented by comprehension work: it is obviously important for these young people to be able to read a passage of prose and to be able to extract information from it, but once again, the comprehension books are either too hard or too childish.

An answer to this problem seems to me to lie in the use of the *Daily Mirror*. This is a popular paper with a huge audience (of every 100,000 school leavers, 40,000 will take this paper).

Its sub-editors, journalists and columnists brilliantly avoid using words that would present difficulty to some of their readers, and there is seldom any obvious impression of over-simplification. Its writers have long experience in putting ideas and policies into everyday language; 33 per cent of its readers try the editorial each day. I do not suggest for a moment that all the *Daily Mirror*'s audience is semi-literate, but there is undoubtedly an awareness in the paper that some readers may have reading difficulty. Taken as a reading exercise for slow learners, it has many advantages.

This is not to say that one merely gives the child a copy of the paper and tells him to get on with it. Reading and comprehension of this sort must be purposive, and at one school Mr John Welch and I inaugurated a scheme in which each pupil was given a weekly question sheet, duplicated beforehand and based on one edition of the paper which the school bought in bulk for that day. The expense was negligible since different classes could easily use the same editions. The question sheets folded neatly into two pages, could be kept in a folder, and formed quite a good diary of news for that term—even though it was the news for only one day a week. We tried to make the questions as interesting and relevant as possible, and after each one we would put the number of the page where each answer could be found. Typical questions for one day would be:

(1) How many strikes were there in 1965 (page 5)?
(2) How much is £100 saved in 1952 worth now (page 11)?
(3) Why was there a strike in Yorkshire yesterday (page 14)?

On the question papers we would leave gaps for the class to complete the answers. If there was a map, we would print it, and the class would fill in details that we had suggested. They would be asked to write out slangy cartoon captions in standard English. Each member of the English department took a turn at writing a question sheet, and when this was known it led to some lively anticipation: what would Mr X's choice of questions be? In this way, the pupils were reading things they enjoyed, and were also gaining confidence by being able to answer simple but useful questions on the information they had gained. It can cause something of a shock to introduce a tabloid news-paper into one's lessons, but the results can be very worthwhile.

CONCLUSION: THE POPULAR AND QUALITY PRESS

Criticising the popular press is almost a national sport; in public and private forums one can hear it condemned now and again by critics who would themselves only consider reading the quality press. There is often a great deal of truth in these criticisms, but they tend on occasions to be one-sided and a little unfair. One can and should criticise a popular paper for distorting the news, but not for using language not normally found in *The Times* or for dealing with topics healthy in them-selves but not to be found in the columns of *The Guardian*. Each paper has the right to its own particular character and audience, so long as what it prints is morally defensible.

In fact, all the different organs of the press have their faults, and although the teacher will probably have his own favourite newspaper, he would be unwise to try to convert all his pupils to reading it. There are of course many things wrong with the popular press, and the teacher should feel at liberty to point them out. In its own way it is extremely patronising; forty years ago, potential reporters were given this advice for 'getting on the right side of the Great British Public', and the picture is not so different today. 'Amuse it. Cheer it up. Chat to it. Bully it a little. Tickle its funny bone. Giggle with it. Confide in it. Give it now and again a good old cry. It loves that.'[1]

No-one would want himself to be manipulated in this de-grading way. Yet the popular press has something to offer, both in what it says and how it says it. It can avoid what Richard Hoggart described as the 'intellectual smugness, spiritual chauvinism and snobbery, and cocktail party polish' of the

---

[1] Michael Joseph, *Journalism for Profit*.

quality press. It aims at and secures an enormous audience, quite beyond the reaches of the quality press. Its ideal purpose has been defined by the Press Council as 'to expose injustices, to right wrongs, to befriend the friendless and to help the helpless. . .they take up causes and run campaigns which would not naturally see the light of day in the staider press.. . . They are invariably on the side of patriotism and legality, of courage and chivalry'.[1]

This may be too rosy a view; one should remember Richard Hoggart's description of them as a 'dolly mixture of facts and bits', and that 'one does not read such papers, one looks at them'. What the teacher can do is to remember that different people require newspapers to serve different purposes; some prefer entertainment as a first priority, while others require news and information. Readers must be given the choice, but before this choice can be really valid, they must know what they are choosing, and what the alternatives are. The teacher can help pupils in this by showing them, through their work, each paper's individual character, which papers report most accurately as well as comprehensively, and which of them do neither of these things. The pupils can then, if they wish, make something of this knowledge into a criterion for judging papers in the future.

In all events, pupils will see the need for as many newspapers as possible when they realise that no one newspaper has a monopoly of the truth. Pupils who may find the interpretative work rather difficult will still enjoy the study, with its practical demands of measuring, compiling and recording, and will learn quite a lot by doing this alone. For the rest, this study may make them more critical of some aspects of the press; I hope it will also teach them to use a newspaper to its fullest extent.

[1] *Second Annual Report of the General Council of the Press*, 1955.

CHAPTER II

ADVERTISING

There is no doubt in my mind that the teacher should be concerned with advertising. To begin with, some £500 m., about 2 per cent of our national income, is spent on advertising, much of it directed at the juvenile market with its very large spending power. In return, Dr Mark Abrams estimated that the British teenager spends nearly 25 per cent of his spending money on clothing, 14 per cent on drink and tobacco, 12 per cent on sweets, soft drinks and snacks, and a good proportion of the rest on entertainment goods. By buying these things many youths feel they are buying their way into the teenage world. How much this is the responsibility of the manufacturers and advertisers is hard to say, but it is perfectly true that one of the chief fears played on in advertisements directed at teenagers is that of being left out and not being properly 'with it'. Not only is there great pressure on the teenager to enter this commercial cult of youth, but once he is in it he is always being urged to renew his stock and stay with the fashion. Of course fashions do change, but one cannot help feeling that occasionally there is something artificial in a fashion that comes and goes so quickly, and that the only real beneficiary is the manufacturer with his constant cash turn-over.

At the moment there is little beyond shrewd commonsense to protect young people against the onslaught of advertisements, and to teach them how to use them to their own advantage. I do not underestimate the commonsense of youth today; as a teacher I am constantly surprised and delighted at it. But one's responsibilities clearly do not stop there. For example, the tobacco manufacturers spend about £20 m. a year on advertising; in 1965 the government contributed £117,000 to combat juvenile smoking. Who is winning the battle: the party with all the money, or the one with the facts, but not the means to distribute them? Obviously the manufacturers are winning hands down, and health is being jeopardised to the same extent as before the report on lung cancer. One-quarter of male smokers start to smoke before they are sixteen.

Tobacco is the most extreme example I can take to show the need for action in the classroom. Yet the methods used to persuade people to smoke are not peculiar to tobacco advertising, and the class can only benefit by understanding how various means of persuasion work over a wide range of goods. Many of these methods I regard as debased and as a real threat to our values. If these lessons seem to become something of a campaign, it needs to be emphasised that our quarrel is only with undesirable advertising. If the class becomes more critical of some advertisements, I hope it will be ready to appreciate the better sort. Implicit in many books critical of advertising is the desire to return to a society which has no advertising, or where it is contained in short informative statements of fact. This clearly is impractical. If we live in a consumer economy it should be an efficient one. Purely informative advertisements do not seem to work over a large field. They have been tried, apparently without success, in Russia. Typical of this is a Russian advertisement for a brassière, reported in an English magazine, which contained a mass of technical detail, but was without any obvious feminine appeal. 'It is unfortunate that in our country intelligent and lively advertising is so rare, and that instead of advertising one comes across unwieldy and dull information, masquerading as advertising while its wording is as dull as ditchwater.' This is Professor Maslov, a Russian, writing in the *Ekonomicheskya Gazette*.[1] He goes on, 'It is impossible to plan consumption, the structure of community turnover, and particularly the prospective family budget, if we do not have planning on demand indexes'. One is reminded of the early Trade Union leader, John Burns: 'The tragedy of the working man is the poverty of his desires'.

[1] Quoted in Harris and Seldon, *Advertising in Action*

Efficient consumer advertising is now an inevitable part of putting new products on the market, and of maintaining mass production, especially against seasonal or other fluctuations in public demand. It can lead to a price reduction should the product sell very well, although this does not happen as often as it might. It encourages the shopkeeper to stock new goods, and it can create a brand name that can generally be trusted for quality where quality is urgently needed. The alternatives are more hawkers and circulars, larger retail margins, or the outright purchase, by manufacturers, of shops in which they can sell their own goods. It is relevant, when thinking of social cost, that advertising subsidises television, newspapers, public transport and cinemas to the extent of about £110 m. per year.

None of these claims, however, should be pressed too hard, although the class should know them. For every worthwhile new product introduced on the market, there may be a ridiculous one. For every sensible modification there may be nothing better than built-in obsolescence. Without advertising for a long time, Marks and Spencer, Boots, and Sainsbury's maintained excellent mass-production techniques. If successful advertising has enabled ball-point pens, for example, to be sold cheaply, it sometimes adds to the cost of a packet of detergent.

Advertisements can have a harmful effect on the product. So far as cleansing quality is concerned, the amount of lather produced by the detergent is quite irrelevant: lather is blather. Nor is whiteness the best criterion for a good wash, as it may involve harmful bleaching. Yet in order to keep up with their advertised image, detergent firms use bleaching powder and 'foam stabilisers'. Which came first: the image or the ignorance? If, however, we agree that advertising is necessary to our sort of society, does this mean that we accept a situation where the individual is like an Amazonian native standing in the library of the British Museum 'with all the members of the staff shouting at him that the books they have are the best . . . while he is searching for the books with the prettiest colours, best pictures, or even the most attractive smells'.[1]

[1] Dr C. D. Harbury in a Fabian pamphlet: *Efficiency and the Consumer*.

Will we end up with J. B. Priestley's Admass: 'my name for the whole system of an increasing productivity, plus inflation, plus high-pressure advertising and salesmanship, plus mass communications, plus cultural democracy, and the creation of the mass mind, the mass man'?[1]

There are dangers, and people in the advertising world are never slow to blame the teachers for the low public taste they, the advertisers, have to cater for. In *Advertising in a Free Society* the authors, Messrs Harris and Seldon, both sympathetic to advertising, say, 'If education has not yet taught everyone to choose wisely, there is no other way for a free society than to try to expedite the process'. Cecil King, of the *Daily Mirror*, is more forthright: 'It is only the people who conduct newspapers and similar organisations who have any idea quite how indifferent, quite how stupid, quite how uninterested in education of any kind the great bulk of the British people are.'[2]

The teacher should be ready to accept these challenges. He must teach his class to understand the appeal of advertisements, to reject those which seem to be hitting below the belt, and to accept those which are trying to do their job in the most acceptable way. He must not ignore the nature of the product advertised; a good advertisement can still advertise a bad product. Here the teacher has strong allies: consumer research organisations. They give the final test of the advertisements' value. I shall discuss how the teacher can use these organisations later; there is no doubt that a wider use of consumer research, which can already reach a British readership of about two million, would benefit our advertising and economy.

Most of the examples we will be studying in class will come from newspapers and magazines, which have two main types of advertisements: classified and display. Classified advertisements, which are generally specific notices, usually in ordinary type size, do not make interesting study material, so we shall concentrate on the display advertisements.

---

[1] *Journey down a Rainbow* (Cresset Press and Heinemann).
[2] National Union of Teachers, *Popular Culture and Personal Responsibility. A Study Outline*.

After the last war there was a general feeling amongst left-wing circles and put into words by George Orwell that 'False optimism was fed to the general public by the gutter press, which lives on its advertisements and is therefore interested in keeping trade conditions normal. Year after year the Beaverbrook press assured us in huge headlines that THERE WILL BE NO WAR, and as late as the beginning of 1939 Lord Rothermere was describing Hitler as "a great gentleman" '.[1] The record is dismal indeed, but the Royal Commission on the Press in 1949 demolished the idea that advertisers actually put *pressure* on papers to keep an optimistic viewpoint. Then, as now, the relationship was far more intangible than this, and evidence on it is difficult to come by.[2] Recently one national newspaper refused to advertise a book on how to stop smoking, while another paper was very slow to mention the adverse report *Which?* made on a cheap and frequently advertised brand of car. *Scrutiny*, the journal of the Advertising Inquiry Council, has built up a dossier on what it calls 'teamwork' between journalists and advertisers, where an article on, say, 'Meals and Men' will be surrounded by advertisements putting forward products favourably mentioned in the text. Other critics complain that 'puffs' on commercial products written and distributed by public relations officers will be reprinted in a paper under the name of a journalist, often with little alteration. Yet few people would ever believe that advertisers have any real say in editorial matter, and given that there may be some indirect control on occasions, which pupils should certainly know and find out about, Orwell was equally right when he wrote in the same book,'I do not suppose there is one paper in England that can be straightforwardly bribed with hard cash'.

---

[1] *The Lion and the Unicorn* (Secker and Warburg).

[2] In 1962, two separate Government Commissions actually disagreed on this. The *Royal Commission on the Press 1961–2* found 'It is difficult to establish proof either way', while the *Final Report of the Committee on Consumer Protection* found 'while we do not allege that editorial columns are corrupted on any great scale by advertising influence,we cannot avoid the conclusion that such an occurrence is by no means unknown.'

THE APPEAL OF ADVERTISEMENTS

There are many ways in which advertisements appeal to the public, and some are far more acceptable than others. Few people would object to an advertisement with an aesthetic or informative appeal; most would also accept humorous and 'reminder' advertisements. But we may feel very differently about the number of advertisements which appeal to a not always very pleasant or intelligent self-interest, or the sort of feelings a good education should be fighting, and which are often quoted as evidence of the moral decline of the young. One can also note the adman's frequent connection of speed with petrol, youth with tobacco, sociability with alcohol, and happiness with material possessions. It would be foolish to blame the adman for the evils of our society, but the very least one can say is that too often he is a positive hindrance to the sort of standards teachers are supposed to inculcate. Besides, no democracy can feel really at ease while the weaknesses of so many are being exploited by so few. Messrs Harris and Seldon put the case for the advertiser who knows he is misleading the public, as follows: 'If a bath soap, a fountain pen, or a carpet give more pleasure when the customer thinks it is used by a duchess or a television performer, then he is making a logical decision in buying it; he is being more sensible than his critics, and the manufacturer and his advertising agent would be wasting their time, the newspaper its space, in giving information about technical composition or performance'.[1] No teacher can feel happy with the idea of his pupils being led off so tamely into a world of illusion and unreal values. When day-dreaming and fantasy, as well as more directly anti-social ideas, are encouraged by advertising, society suffers, as well as the consumer's purse.

The best way to make children alive to this situation is to show them the specific appeals that lie behind many advertisements, and then to discuss whether these appeals are helpful to

[1] *Advertising in Action.*

us as individuals and to society as a whole. Thus one will condemn those that appeal to herd-instinct, snobbishness, ignorance, envy and possessiveness, and one will question advertisements that appeal to honest and good human feelings in order to make them spill over on to the quite irrelevant product that the advertiser is trying to sell. According to St Augustine, the beginning of moral regeneration lies in conceiving an aversion, but it should be obvious that merely making pupils dislike undesirable advertising appeals is only half the teacher's battle. If pupils are going to turn away from phoney or vicious appeals, they must have as their criteria, as far as is possible, the real and the good. Otherwise 'we run the risk of not giving the students a fair chance, of unnecessarily hurting or embarrassing them, and worst of all, of encouraging the "debunking spirit", the "spirit that denies". In proscribing sentimentality we may inhibit a sincere emotion; one would prefer even some spilling over of emotion to the sour "knowing-ness" which can be induced'.[1]

The class and the teacher can spend some time accumulating a basic list of human appeals favoured by advertisers, and can subject each one to a judgement arrived at through discussion. This method is open to criticism: many of the motivations in advertising are inextricably mixed; some advertisements will fall outside the net anyhow. Nevertheless, I have found the following list and examples, which I have grouped into rough categories, the best way of showing how children and their parents are being 'got at'.

1. *By appealing to physical comfort*

(a) *Appealing to greed*

'More than a treat—a food.' This slogan is meant to make you believe that something extra to your normal diet—an indulgence—is good for you, and therefore all right. Guilt feelings over greediness are thus stilled. Its variants are often

[1] Richard Hoggart, *Teaching Literature* (National Institute of Adult Education).

used for things which have little nutritive value. Of this slogan Elizabeth Gundrey[1] points out that the proteins, vitamins, and minerals in ice-cream are negligible, and the calories could be found in one ounce of chocolate. 'You owe yourself a luxury' is yet another attempt to overcome the remnants of a Puritan conscience and persuade us that what we eat through greed is really good for us. This appeal is often used for alcohol, sweets, and ice-cream.

There are many other examples in advertising where the copywriter seizes on the aspect of the product most open to suspicion and vigorously defends it. Why else should frozen food be called 'Fresher than fresh'? Tins of 'Fresh garden peas' would be better labelled 'Cheap field peas', perhaps grown on a plantation abroad. A greengrocer never has to advertise his goods in this way; they speak for themselves. Again, 'Farm House Bread, made from the cream of the wheat, with that true country flavour' (in fact, mass-produced and steam-baked with ordinary flour in Bermondsey).[2]

(b) Appealing to the wish for ease and comfort

Sometimes these advertisements can usefully bring some labour-saving device to public attention. On the other hand, they often help the consumer to justify his ease and comfort to himself, before going on to suggest improvements in it: 'You need a Trust House Holiday'. Having established this arbitrary need, we go on to hear about 'good food, good surroundings, and a really good rest'. Sometimes the ease is nothing short of miraculous. Dirty marks 'disappear in a flash' from baths. 'Just sprinkle' is quite enough. Although advertisers are warned by the British Code of Standards not to use words like 'magic' or 'miracle' this applies strictly only to advertisements for medicine. They are used freely elsewhere, and we must agree that the effect claimed is magical: we hear about the maximum effect with the minimum effort. Whether these modern miracles work, the class will have to decide.

[1] *Your Money's Worth.*
[2] Quoted in *Scrutiny*, III.

2. *By appealing to feelings about health*

It is difficult not to believe that by appealing to a widespread fear of losing health many of these advertisements create, or at least encourage, obsession with the 'ailments' they describe. 'Even ... as early as 25, dry skin tension can age You.' As with 'enlarged pores', 'night starvation' and 'dry scalps', one can only say that if these things do exist, people have been living with them quite happily since Adam. Is it really a good sign when counter sales at chemists' shops assume such vast proportions as they do now? The social consequences of ill health and nervous strain are lovingly played upon. 'An hour under the mistletoe and nothing happened.' 'How did you get to be an old maid, Auntie?' The British Code of Standards' statement on patent-medicine advertising has the effect of pushing proprietary-medicine advertisements far into the realms of the fantastic, where mythical diseases with mythical consequences are first thought up, and then innocuous medicines are found to cure them. 'No advertisement should contain any matter which can be regarded as an offer of medicine or product for, or advice relating to the treatment of serious diseases, complaints, conditions, indications or symptoms which should rightly receive the attention of a registered medical practitioner.' Few people had ever worried about constipation until advertisers took up the story. In this way real illnesses are avoided, and relevant symptoms are not discussed. Instead we have the supremely irrelevant 'The acid in your stomach could burn a hole in your carpet', together with figures on how many beats our hearts give in one day. The class can be set as composition, 'Are we a nation of hypochondriacs?'.

3. *By appealing to social fears and hopes*

(a) *Snob appeal*

This is often used when advertising things consumers use in public, such as newspapers, cigarettes, furniture, cars, clothes, liquor, books, tableware, and some sorts of foods. 'Cigarettes can tell you quite a bit about a man. Men of judgement appreciate Churchman's No 1.' 'Top people take *The Times*' (not, notice, 'well-informed', 'skilled' or 'valuable' people— merely 'top'). Sometimes this snob appeal is frankly inflationary: 'Damnably expensive shirts'.

(b) Identification with famous people

Endorsement by a film star or a sportsman is quite irrelevant to one's own decision, and these testimonials are always paid for. Even if the advertised figure does use the hair oil he says he uses, it is most unlikely he pays the full retail price for it. Identification of this sort is a very primitive mental habit, and children can be encouraged to debunk it. Even sillier are products which claim they are used by people 'in the know'. 'Wonderful bread—bakers eat it.' Undoubtedly, a few bakers do, but then so do a few dustmen. These claims are never accompanied by any figures.

(c) Appealing to the fear of nonconformity

This appeal makes an interesting contrast with the appeal to snobbishness. Sometimes advertisers manage to include both in one: 'A book for the few—120th thousand'. The class can try to establish in what ways people like to be similar, and where they like to compete with their neighbours. Children are thought fair game for this particular appeal. 'Lonely because her straight hair has made her unattractive and unwanted', reads an American advertisement over the face of a wistful child. The answer—a special child's perm. The fear engendered by 'Someone isn't using Amplex' was so genuine that the advertisers were able to reproduce the picture without any copy. Men, too, make their appearance in these pictures, and significantly the male deodorant trade has started flourishing during recent years. In America, this fear of nonconformity has been taken to extreme lengths: in one advertisement, any man who dares to use buttons instead of the zip to fasten his trousers is categorised, with the help of suitable illustration of an embarrassing moment, as INEXCUSABLE![1] How many of these fears are real, and how many are invented by advertisments in order to sell a cure?

(d) Exploiting the fear of losing a job or other people's affection

'Are you easy to get on with? You might well say, "Well, I'm as easy to get on with as the next person". But would your family agree?' Many advertisements follow this line, and Horlicks, for example, have been painting dramatic pictures for some time of stress at home or at the office miraculously cured 'Thanks to Horlicks'.

(e) Bringing in sex appeal

Advertisements may concentrate on achievements or failures with the opposite sex. This is a topic adolescents can talk about with some authority. Their reasons for success are often very different from those found in advertisements. The failures are obviously more delicate matters, and the teacher must be very careful not to intrude into any private unhappiness. Advertisers with a product to sell are not so scrupulous. 'How long since this happened to you?' demands an advertisement, showing masculine hands running caressingly through a woman's hair. This seems aimed at the lonely and unattractive, who cannot draw much comfort from the question or the remedy: another hair shampoo.

4. *By appealing to maternal feelings*

A mother's feelings for her family can be exploited. It is obviously permissable to play on this when advertising diphtheria inoculations or safety in the home, but it is not a feeling to be played on lightly. 'How many days will your child miss this term? Tackle the problem now. Give your family Seven Seas Cod Liver Oil.' There are some advertisements of that sort

[1] Quoted in Turner, *The Shocking History of Advertising.*

46

which go even further, and try to stir up guilt, not fear. 'Mummy, will you play with me sometimes?' 'Mummy, why don't you ever dress up?' The remedy in both cases, Johnson's Wax, which is supposed to prevent time wasted through polishing by hand, obviously will not solve this sort of family problem.

5. *By appealing to housewifely virtues*

(a) *Appealing to the wish to economise*

This is a thoroughly sensible appeal, and it should be encouraged. It is often coupled with a 'windfall' appeal, which is not so healthy. Thus we are often told of the competition we may win, or the vouchers we can collect, if we move quickly; limited availability is always a feature of this sort of advertising. 'Cheaper than ever' is still not a reason for buying something if we do not really want it. A 2/- detergent packet with 3d knocked off is still not *cheaper* than another brand costing 1/9. And how much is there in the packet?

(b) *Appealing to the desire for security and dependability*

This appeal is often accompanied by symbols which express the same feeling: oak trees, the countryside, piles of money. The advertising copy often assumes a dignified swell. Parallel, of course, is the fear of insecurity; balding men without pensions, tyres that explode, houses that burn down. Recently there has been a growth in advertising by banks and the Stock Exchange, who exploit the same market. Brand names, which have given long and useful service, often point this out in their slogans: 'a name you can trust'. This is often true, but the Continental margarine, which made many people ill and killed two, had a very well known brand name. Recently more than three million oil stoves from reputable firms were found to be unsafe, after a distressing series of accidents with young children or the elderly. Liberty is not the only thing that needs constant vigilance.

6. *By appealing through reason*

(a) *Appealing to science*

Here, the science department will have to help with claims for 'revitalised blood', 'extra nourishment to brain and body tissues', and any other new 'wonder' ingredient like the recent curious vogue for chlorophyll. The British Code of Standards relating to the advertising of medicines and treatment forbids advertisements that 'claim to cure any ailment or symptoms of ill health, or contain words or expressions used to imply the extirpation of a disease'. This does not seem to allow patent medicines much scope, yet they are among the most frequently advertised. One way is to substitute the word 'relief' for 'cure'. The class should examine the many ways in which they avoid the letter of the law.

(b) *Appealing to history and tradition*

Most wine and spirits advertisements seem to stress these factors when talking about the mystique of blending, quality and dependability. This is often reinforced by printing the message in heavy Gothic type. 'The same as mother used to have', is a frequent theme for some domestic goods. This is of course in complete contrast to the other cry of 'new' and 'modern'. There are many other contrasting appeals in advertising: economy and extravagance; conformity and social climbing; hopes and fears; English made and foreign glamour. When paired together, such advertisements make amusing comparisons and show quite clearly that advertising never talks with one voice, and contradicts itself so often that there is yet another reason to scrutinise advertising claims most carefully.

(c) *Appealing through facts*

These advertisements are difficult to categorise. Bird's Custard Powder, for instance, gives recipes in its advertisements for different uses of the powder. Other advertisements may tell us facts about the product which really help us to decide whether to buy it or not. The class must learn to discriminate between sensible and superlative claims, relevant and irrelevant facts. McVities have advertisements headed 'When you buy biscuits, look for the weight on the packet— price alone can be deceptive'. Unlike information about a 'wonder drug', this is an observation we can at least appreciate and assess for ourselves.

7. By appealing through 'motivational' research

Some advertisements, pioneered in America, are supposed to appeal to the unconscious, and are usually arrived at through 'depth' interviews where people are asked to recall their feelings about a certain product. If a pattern emerges, the psychologist in charge will recommend that it be built into the advertisement. For instance, free association, and perhaps a certain amount of crude commonsense, disclosed that people were not buying prunes, which were associated with old age and constipation. The new advertisement, which was claimed as a great success, went like this:

> Get them up for the day,
> The bright hearty way,

Tender plump prunes from California—nothing beats a breakfast that starts with the wonder fruit. Prunes taste so bright and sunshiny, and what a wonderful helping of health for the day. Energy-rich fruit sugar...protective vitamins... body-building minerals. (For many folks too, prunes provide just the mild aid to regularity they need to feel their fittest.)

All this went with a cartoon of a mother and family, with the caption: 'How they thrive on prunes, the Californian wonderfruit'.

Here are some other 'discoveries' derived from depth interviews:

(a) Colds: These can mean the person needs attention and security.

(b) Flour is seen as something essentially pure and white, and this must be emphasised in advertisements, even though off-white flour is just as good.

(*c*) People who buy expensive lingerie are often seeking self-gratification. Thus lingerie advertisements usually have an individual appeal. There is often an attractive model who merely poses beside the name of the manufacturer. There is no need to bring in any social message, such as the added sex appeal.

(*d*) People who buy cough sweets really like sweets, but rationalise this feeling into a desire for good health. Thus cough sweets should taste as nice as possible, but the advertisement should stress how effective they are.

(*e*) Women feel guilty about buying ready-made cake mixtures, but buy them through lack of confidence. Thus advertisements should emphasise the impossibility of failure, but should not increase the customer's guilt by stressing how easy it all is.

These are just examples from what is apparently an expanding field. Such hypotheses are made with the aid of word-association tests: 'closure', where the consumer is asked to put his own word into a slogan such as 'Dunlop tyres are——'; Thematic Apperception Tests (TAT for short), where the consumer looks at a picture involving the product and says whatever comes to mind; and story completion, a lengthier version of the closure method. Since many of these techniques closely resemble parlour games, there is no harm in the class trying a little of its own depth interviewing, provided that no one takes it too seriously and it is very near the end of term. The most frequent unconscious motives researchers maintain they find are:

(*a*) Narcissism—love turned back on oneself.

(*b*) Oral gratification—an infantile desire to suck things.

(*c*) Guilt—the anxiety which makes people want to do one thing because they fear that secretly they wish to do another.

(*d*) Image building—the role one creates for oneself.

(*e*) Status symbol—something that increase one's position in society, such as a flashy car, even if this means that you go short on some of the necessities of life.

We have already met most of these desires and feelings in a conscious form; and perhaps their chief interest is that so many *advertisers* believe in their unconscious value, and this helps produce advertisements a little more subtle than the thoroughly old-fashioned: 'Ladies, your neighbours will think you spent more than 16/9 on this shoe'.[1]

These seem to be the main categories, although new ones may crop up during the study. The class always enjoys discussing them, and can generally cap the teacher's examples with better ones from its own experience. When all the categories have been agreed upon, pupils can concentrate on collecting examples of each, and sticking them in their books or folders. This gives the teacher enough material to work on for some time. When this subject is exhausted, he can then go on to other aspects of advertising.

THE WORDING OF ADVERTISEMENTS

In most New York subway stations there is a weighing machine that also tells your fortune. On the side of the machine is printed: 'Weigh your fate'. Generations of New York teenagers have seen comic possibilities in this, and in most cases have erased the 'e' in *fate*. This makes the invitation more accurate, but unpleasing to the manufacturers. Copywriters must always be careful that their slogans do not carry unforeseen possibilities of emendation.

This is a minor consideration when writing copy. The primary need is to attract the reader from the jungle of news and pictures on a printed page, and then hold his attention. This is done either by the copy or the picture. If it is the copy, then the headline must make a strong bid for our attention. It may be through curiosity: 'Are you playing fair with your wife?'; 'How a strange accident saved me from baldness'; 'Men who "know it all" are not invited to read this'; or use of words like 'remarkable', 'sensational', and 'amazing'. It may appeal to our self-interest: 'Retire at 35'; 'To young men who want to

[1] Quoted in *Culture and Environment*

get ahead'. A headline may promise us some news we want to hear: 'New features on Ford trucks', or use phrases like 'important development' or 'the truth about'. A highly successful American advertiser thinks headlines can also be strengthened by the inclusion of emotional words like 'darling', 'love', 'fear', 'proud', 'friend', and 'baby'. When the headline has attracted our initial attention, the copy takes over. There are various key words that often crop up: New! Now! At last! Announcing! If it is about a new product, the copy is often at pains to be specific: 'Beginning July 1', 'Ten days only'. The tense is generally in the present, and the favourite pronoun is the second person plural. The price is usually mentioned—especially if it is reduced—and if enquiries are wanted, it will be emphasised that any enquiry is quite free and carries no obligation whatsoever. This kind of copy is known as 'the hard sell', a mixture of strident urgent terms plus a vigorous recommendation. It often employs its own grammar and vocabulary: yummy, tangy, zippy, chewy, crispy, crunchy, turvy, and tossy. Its facts are forthright but sometimes questionable. 'Doctors in over a thousand skin tests proved this soap makes your skin younger, softer, lovelier than ever.' One would like to know what the tests were, what criterion was used to test 'loveliness', whether the doctors were in the employ of the advertisers, and whether any other brand of soap was used as a control. Similarly, we want to know more about 'bread that is eight times more good for you than any other', chocolate that is 'seven times less fattening than ordinary chocolate', motor oil which 'reduces engine wear by 80 per cent'. These miracles of modern dietetics and technology should certainly do something more to justify their extraordinary claims. The code governing advertising lays down that no advertisements should have any 'intent to mislead'. If the class thinks the code is being broken in this case, unless of course these claims are true, it will probably be able to find other examples of this fairly quickly.

To evade this suspicion, an American has perfected in his advertisements 'the philosophy of the uncheckable claim'.

Thus he can say of one of his products 'Doctors use it'. It is almost certain that at least one doctor does. Another product adds 'zip', a third will 'light up your home with joy'. With this philosophy went another one: each product must have a 'unique selling proposition'. Thus, of beer bottles, they are 'washed in live steam'. Now all bottles are washed in steam, whether live or dead it is difficult to say. It happens to be the standard procedure for washing bottles. But by saying it first, the advertiser has made a claim for his product which no other advertiser can copy, because if they do they will only reflect the glory of the product that first used the claim. To put it differently, any detergent advertiser who mentions 'brightness' in his copy will inadvertently be advertising Omo which is now linked with the slogan 'Omo adds brightness'. Hard-sell copy is generally written in short violent bursts. The class should discover what types of product it is generally associated with.

The 'soft sell' uses a different method, which aims not so much at thrusting facts down your throat, but rather at surrounding the product with the sort of atmosphere which will make you want to buy it. Thus toilet paper will be advertised not by any reference to its use, price and volume, but by pictures and a text recalling soft autumnal shades, or by an image of being 'the perfect hostess'—people in advertisements still go to house-parties. In motor advertising there may be less mention of a car's gear-box than the idea of seeing the world when you have a car. In the background, a rickshaw boy is trotting past . . . Through it all runs the idea of establishing a favourable brand image, so that soap is associated with romance, beer with strength, and hats with business acumen. The danger here is that product and image become fused, and purchasers are persuaded that they can buy an experience as well as the box of chocolates, or masculine virility as well as a packet of cigarettes. Apart from being obvious confidence tricks, these advertisements debase our language. Words which once stood for real feelings and attitudes are now bandied about to produce a favourable brand image. Once again, the teacher can do very little in this type of lesson unless he has helped his class to have some idea about what emotions and the words describing them can really mean. Occasionally, brand images change: Player's cigarettes used to be advertised by a bearded sailor, who suddenly changed into two young things in a country setting. The class should be encouraged to comment on the significance of changes like these. If the teacher reads out some 'soft-sell' copy without mentioning the product, it will soon be obvious how far away from reality the copy has become, since it is sometimes impossible to guess the product. A lot of bad fiction, noticeably in the women's weekly magazines, closely resembles this sort of overblown sentiment. This should be pointed out to the class, and the teacher should read some clear and direct prose as a contrast.

Soft-sell advertisements do not deal solely with sentiment. Some, by using a high-flown literary style, try to establish a mood of extreme respectability. These advertisements generally appear in quality papers, either for prestige purposes, or to advertise expensive consumer goods, like alcohol, clothes and even note-paper. At other times they might not even mention the product, but will merely ensure that the name and image of the firm comes across favourably. One series of advertisements showed pictures of the countryside with the legend underneath 'We do not advertise in places like these'. Not all are so short and to the point as this. At their worst they use what George Orwell called the 'inflated style'. 'A mass of Latin words falls upon the facts like snow, blurring the outlines and covering up all details. The great enemy of clear language is insincerity. When there is a gap between one's real and one's declared aims, one turns as it were instinctively to long words and exhausted idioms, like cuttlefish squirting out ink.'[1]

Steering a middle course between the hard and soft sell are the reminder campaigns, whose effect lies in the reiteration of a good slogan and which are still the backbone of advertising.

[1] *Critical Essays* (Secker and Warburg).

'My Goodness, my Guinness', 'Players please', and other tags, usually just as alliterative, have become part of our vocabularies. Since the slogan generally remains the same, the variation tends to lie in the accompanying design. It may be a new picture, or a new joke; and some of them can be really amusing. Since these campaigns tend to give little information about the product, they can be looked at far more in terms of design. Are they pleasant to look at, or would they spoil the ugliest hoarding? Would we enjoy them in some locations, but not in others? Recently the advertising industry has been more strict with advertisers who clutter up town and the country with badly-placed posters and bill-boards, and it is a good thing for pupils to know about this, and the powers of the advertisers' own 'clutter code'.

By now pupils should be able to show they know the difference between hard and soft sells, and they should also be able to spot a brand image. There are many other exercises. Are certain words always linked to certain goods? What are the key advertising words that seem to appear everywhere? How many uncheckable claims can the class find? Find some writing, either in advertising or cheap fiction, which uses the inflated style, and comment on the vocabulary and images it uses. Can you find any more neologisms to add to the list?

THE LAYOUT OF ADVERTISEMENTS

An advertisement is usually composed of an illustration, a heading, copy and a logotype, which is the name of the firm paying for the advertisement. Usually the illustration or the copy is given chief emphasis by the designer. The illustration often has the same tendency as soft-sell copy: quite arbitrary connections are established between two irrelevant subjects. A Zurich newspaper recently banned an advertisement comparing a statue of Venus with a modern car, on the grounds that no arbitrary link should be made with historical, political, or cultural factors which bear no relation to the product. Compared with some of our advertisements, the relationships

5   55

objected to here seemed quite mild. Situations of real emotions —a mother looking at her child, a couple getting married—are linked with beverages and hair shampoos. This in its way is as dangerous as debasing historical and cultural subjects, though in so far as the emotion generated by such illustrations spills over on to the product, they probably make for very effective advertisement.

There are many types of illustration. It may be a large photograph or a drawing. The drawings are required by law not to give a misleading account of the article, and the camera 'cannot lie'. Nevertheless, distortion still takes place. A small refrigerator looks much bigger if a very small female model is photographed standing beside it. Like verbal headings, the illustration is often made provocative, in this case by showing something in unusual perspective, or by 'cropping' the photograph (cutting it off at an unexpected point). It may be an illustration of interest to a specialised group: motorists would look twice at a picture showing someone turning a steering wheel with one finger. Subjects usually certain to create general interest include babies, brides, animals, famous people, people in odd situations, and pictures that tell a story, especially if it is a romantic one.

The optical centre of an advertisement—the place where we tend to focus our attention—is in the middle of the layout one-third of the way above the horizontal centre of the advertisement. Many advertisements begin their copy at about this point. The illustration is often linked to the copy by a common background, or one overlaps the other. Modern advertisements tend to use more white space than before, and do not insist on the old-fashioned formal balance, where all the main elements of the picture are at the centre. Instead, we now have advertisements full of colour and movement, with little formal balancing of left against right, top against bottom. At their best, such advertisements can give some aesthetic pleasure, and there is everything to be said for the class collecting the best of them. Other items for collecting can be illustrations which are misleading in the way mentioned before: bikini girls advertising garden rollers; the Great Wall of China advertising toilet paper.

ADVERTISEMENTS AND MEDIA SELECTION

In 1963 £5 m. was spent on cinema advertising, £15 m. on outside advertising, £16 m. on posters and transport, £85 m. on television advertising, £234 m. on press advertising as well as £146 m. on catalogues and leaflets, window and interior display, exhibitions, free samples and gifts, administration and radio advertising. Which service does the advertiser choose, and why? His advertisement has to be shown in the right medium and in the right place in order to get its maximum effect. For example, advertisements shown during cinema programmes do best if they are of exciting teenage subjects like glamour or motorbikes, because 80 per cent of cinema audiences are teenagers, who often go to the cinema as a form of escape. The cinema is no longer a family concern, and thus there are fewer generalised advertisements. Advertisements in the underground railways have been found to be most effective when aimed at young people of the lower middle class, such as office workers and shop assistants. The reason incidentally why so many lingerie advertisements are to be found on escalators is not that tube travellers have an abnormal interest in this subject, but because the moving staircase makes it difficult for the amateur artist to add embellishments or comments. Posters on hoardings are aimed at everybody, and should have a simple message, as many people pass them quickly in cars. The end of the hoarding is considered to be the best place for an advertisement, and accordingly it costs more to hire. Advertisements on the outside of buses are aimed at the world in general and at motorists in particular; inside a bus the advertisements often concentrate on housewives.

In newspapers, the best and most expensive place for advertisements is 'solus' on the page, with no competition from other advertisements. Second best is to share the page with one other advertisement: semi-solus. The 'ear spaces' at the top of the front page, on each side of the newspaper's title, are also highly prized. At all events, an advertisement is best placed if it is 'next matter', which is when it borders on an actual piece of news. This means there is more chance that the eye will stray from the news to the advertisement. Thus the front page is the best, as the news there is most widely read. It may help if the matter on the page has something in common with the advertisements, so we find women's advertisements on the women's page, and beer and pools advertisements on the sports page, almost entirely read by men. The choice of day can also be important: Monday is good for drapery and fashion advertisements, since women are ready to do some luxury shopping, but Thursday and Friday are the days for stocking up for the week-end, and there are more grocery advertisements. Saturday is the relaxed day, so there are mail order advertisements to skim through, and week-end hobbies like gardening are catered for.

When newspapers wish to sell advertising space, they tend to emphasise either the 'quality' of their readers or their quantity. This information is gauged by the annual *National Readership Surveys* of the Institute of Practitioners in Advertising (see also Appendix B.). When assessing whether a reader is an A, B, C, D or E type the following definitions are used:

Social Grade	Social Status	Occupations	Income likely to be
A	Upper middle-class	Higher managerial, administrative or professional	Over £2,000
B	Middle-class	Intermediate managerial, administrative or professional	£1,000–£2,000
C1	Lower middle-class	Supervisory or clerical, junior managerial or professional	Under £1,000
C2	Skilled working class	Skilled manual worker	£14–£22 weekly
D	Working class	Semi-skilled worker	£6.10–£14 weekly
E	Those at lowest level of subsistence	Pensioners, widows, casual workers	Under £6.10 weekly

A social breakdown of the adult reading population in Great Britain gives us:

A, B	5,066,000	C2	14,786,000
C1	7,251,000	D, E	12,796,000

IPA National Readership Surveys Jan.–Dec. 1965

Class groupings are notoriously difficult to make, but these are roughly the size of the different markets the advertiser is aiming at. A, B men often read *The Times, The Guardian,* and *Financial Times.* A, B women often read *Vogue, Queen,* and theatre programmes. Thus the advertisements in these publications will tend to be A, B in tone. Although these people read other publications, they will not be the main section of the public to do so, and therefore there are few A, B advertisements in papers read widely by the D, E sector; this is particularly true of prestige advertisements. In trade journals, newspapers use these figures as a bait to attract advertisers: '*Radio Times* provides the highest A, B, C1 coverage of any single press medium' plus a picture of a well-dressed couple silhouetted against a comfortable gabled house. 'The *Daily Mirror* has 15 m. readers, almost 8 m. of whom are skilled workers and their families', implies that not all its readers are of the D, E class.

Thus we already have important clues as to which class the advertisement is really for. We can guess fairly accurately the class, sex, income, and some of the social habits of the potential consumer aimed at by the advertiser. Many questions suggest themselves. Are the snobbish advertisements aimed at the A, B readers, who are intent on maintaining their standards, or at the C readers, encouraging them to climb the social scale? Does one class seem to suffer more from fear than another? Are there such things as 'class' products: Jaguar cars for A, B readers only, and patent medicine advertisements for the D, E readers? Is there any other significant difference between A, B advertising and the rest? Do their tastes, aspirations and needs differ from the C, D, E readers? Any discussion of class boundaries is bound to be tricky, but in so far as advertisers treat people differently in different papers, it must be a factor in our examination. Applied sociology can do no harm, unless the teacher implies a value judgement on what are still loosely called the 'upper' and 'lower' classes.

CLASSWORK ON ADVERTISING

Some of the basic projects to do with advertising have already been described. There are many others possible, which can have an equally stimulating effect. For example, the teacher must always remember that a good advertisement cannot excuse a bad product, and for this reason he must introduce the class to the whole field of consumer research. If we wish for a society with good advertisements for good products, it is short-sighted to criticise advertisements alone. This is particularly true of expensive goods. If someone is misled into buying a bad cheap product, he need not make the same mistake next time. But expensive goods have to last, and it is essential that the advertisers and the manufacturers should realise this and show a sense of public responsibility. A quick way for the class to discover more about this is to read a copy of *Which?*. One can choose a survey of some expensive product, and exhibit the findings, paying special concern to the product nominated as 'best buy' and the products not recommended. Then advertisements for all the products should be collected. When the dossier is complete, we can find out whether the advertisement for the 'best buy' product made the most of it, and what the advertisement for the 'worst buy' goods managed to say about them. Elizabeth Gundrey has made a list of misleading claims compared with her organization's researches.[1]

Perhaps the class can help with some examples from their own homes. Occasionally the illustration is misleading, especially

[1] *Your Money's Worth.*

Product	Claim	*Shopper's Guide* Findings
Ironing board	Superior finish	Rough wood, nail heads exposed, tacks rusty
Grater	High-grade Steel	Tin-plated mild steel
Glue	Incomparable strength	Join parted under a strain of 182 lbs. Other adhesives reached 364–555 lbs.

those on the covers of cheap paper-back books, where, to quote a parody, *Oliver Twist* might be unsuitably illustrated under the caption, 'Insatiable—he had to have more'.

Consumer research does not mean that the shopper need never think again. If a firm is given a particularly bad report, it may modify its goods very quickly. The best way to buy an expensive object is still to have it on a period of free trial. If the pupil thinks his home contains at least one really excellent product, he should try to write his own advertisement for it, which should be as helpful and objective as he can manage. In general, though, I do not think it is a good idea to ask a class to design its own advertisements. One cannot expect pupils to boost other people's products, and the exercise often becomes merely facetious. Perhaps an exception can be made for issues affecting the class. A period spent designing and writing an advertisement about a school society, road safety, litter, juvenile smoking, or a school trip need not be wasted. It is an opportunity to use some of the more acceptable techniques the class has been learning about.

Adolescents are naturally interested in the advertisements aimed at the teenage market, particularly in pin-up magazines and cheap romantic picture stories. It is perhaps one of the best chances a teacher has to point the differences between illusion and reality. Both the advertisements and the fiction often promise a dreamy bliss in the arms of a handsome dark stranger; the 'Can I help you?' column on another page tells a different, often rather sad story. The class can write two dialogues: between two typical teenagers, and between two typical advertisement teenagers. The difference is of course enormous, and very amusing. Variants on this topic for composition are: A trip to Advertland; If all the advertisements came true; If someone believed all the advertisements he saw. Another title which goes down well (unpredictably) is: The advertising campaign that got out of hand.[1]

---

[1] For further discussion on composition topics, see my 'Choosing Compositions', in *English versus Examinations* edited by Brian Jackson (Chatto and Windus), 1965.

Typical goods advertised for teenagers are clothes, cosmetics, entertainments, sweets, soft drinks, motor scooters and record players. The class should pay special attention to the arguments used in the copy, and ask itself: 'What is the adman's idea of a teenager? What are the key words which usually crop up? Do some advertisements ever appear to encourage teenage behaviour commonly deplored in the same paper, like drunkenness, promiscuity, heavy smoking, motor-bike accidents through speeding?'. Here again, a dossier would help: the class can keep a record of news and court sentences quoted against teenagers, and can try to find advertisements which may be encouraging the very same behaviour.

It is quite an exciting process to follow an advertisement campaign through from start to finish. Trade papers like the *Advertiser's Weekly* and the *Advertiser's Review* will print prior information like 'Murray and Sons are going to use large spaces in the *Daily Mirror*, the *Daily Express*, and *Sunday Mirror* throughout June for Erinmore Tobacco'. They will often print the 'keynote' to the campaign, 'Shoes which make it fun to have feet'. When the campaign begins, the class can collect different examples of it, and can decide on the intended audience, the motivation, and the visual and social quality of the advertisement. There are some useful technical hints on how to judge an advertisement in the weekly notes of the *Advertiser's Review*; these are particularly helpful on professional errors in layout, design, and occasionally wording. The *Advertiser's Weekly* in its column 'At a glance guide' announces enough campaigns each week for every pupil to have something to keep him fairly busy. The trade advertisements in these papers make an interesting comparison with the same companies' consumer advertisements. It is strange to hear *Woman*, normally so demure, telling its trade colleagues that its '8,380,000 customers are *conditioned* to delight in colour, so why waste your colour advertising on men?'. *Punch* is advertised not as a humorous weekly, but as 'the positive plus in space buying, with the most loyal readership in publishing today'.

The usual standard of advertising is generally very high, and both papers make a point of printing miniature copies of what they consider the most attractive advertisements of the week.

There are many more tricks of the trade which will interest the class. One of the advertisers' chief problems is how to create the white pea in the pod, or, in other words, how to persuade customers that almost identical products such as brands of oil or detergent have any real differences at all. Products like these always demand ingenuity in the advertiser, sometimes with doubtful wisdom, as with Shell's emphasis on speed. The best and worst advertisements often come when two products are nearly indistinguishable: a difference is created either by shock tactics or by inventing a favourable—and perhaps a cheerful—brand image. Facts cannot help very much, as they are almost identical too. Other advertisements to watch are those concerned with products which are still fairly new on the mass market: baby food, soft drinks, carpets, furniture, central heating, lawn-mowers, scooters, record players, holidays abroad, country houses, banks and the Stock Exchange. The sale of these products is still expanding, and in most cases brand images have still to be created. There is as yet little product pattern; no constant association of the same ideas with the same products, such as whiteness with detergents, ostracism without deodorants and manliness with beer.

Writing in the *New Statesman and Nation*, Miss Marghanita Laski once made up an unlikely slogan: 'Cheap clothes for fat old women', and then paraphrased it neatly into advertising jargon as 'Limited income clothes for dignified maturity'. There are indeed many euphemisms and half truths in advertising, and most pupils will be able to produce something as stark as Miss Laski's re-writing. It has been suggested that in advertising terms 'delicate membrane' means any part of the body, and 'pure deep cleansing' means washing one's face. 'Exclusive' means expensive, and to last a 'lifetime' means until the next model is produced. 'Harsh irritants' are only found in a rival's brand of detergent, whilst 'highest quality', 'finest ingredients', and 'packed under best conditions' mean almost nothing. Words found in many contexts but with little objective meaning include 'flavour', 'service', 'new', 'fast' and 'satisfying'.

One project of great relevance to any class is an examination of tobacco advertising. Pupils should first be reminded that deaths from lung cancer are still increasing, and incidence of this disease is proportional to the amount of cigarettes smoked. This is to say nothing of the bronchial, digestive and heart trouble smoking may also bring about. A small anti-smoking campaign has been started by the Ministry of Health, and although its posters are now accepted, it got off to a bad start by the refusal of the British Poster Advertisers' Association to exhibit the first campaign poster. This was ostensibly because the poster—which showed a cigarette whose smoke formed the word 'cancer'—was misleading, since one cigarette is unlikely to cause this disease. If this is misleading, then so are very many other posters that the B.P.A. exhibits quite cheerfully.

There is evidence that the tobacco manufacturers made a special bid for the juvenile market a few years ago. Certainly, there was a spate of advertisements emphasising the youth and charm of people who smoke, even though the majority of smokers are over thirty. This got to such a pitch that Parliament was asked to intervene, and eventually an agreement was reached between the I.T.A. and the tobacco industry on television cigarette advertising. This stipulated that no cigarette advertisements should be shown until 9 o'clock, by which time some children at any rate will have gone to bed. It also agreed that no advertisement should be screened greatly over-emphasising the pleasures of smoking, or featuring the conventional heroes of the young, or appealing to pride and manliness, or strikingly presenting romantic situations and young people in love in such a way as to seem to link the pleasure of such situations with the pleasures of smoking.[1]

This seems to leave the advertiser with very little leeway, but

[1] Following further parliamentary action, no advertisements concerning smoking are to appear on I.T.V. after 31 July 1965.

as always he will come through, and he may even infringe some of these self-negotiated limiting clauses. Of course he gets free advertising every time an actor in a television play lights a cigarette, an action often written into the script by unimaginative directors who are seeking some facile way of breaking up a stream of dialogue. A fairly new advertising gimmick is vouchers in cigarette packets for 'free gifts'. Thus after smoking 36,000 cigarettes there is, besides anything else you may pick up, a free refrigerator waiting for you. To gain these large gifts, one will obviously have to start smoking young—and hard. Pupils should monitor tobacco advertising very carefully, and if they find that the rules are being broken they should report to the class.

There may be cases, as in the study of newspapers, where a teacher and his class might want to take further action about what they considered to be a really dishonest or undesirable advertisement. Provided this opportunity for action is not abused, it can be an excellent training in democratic rights, which are so rarely invoked because of the ignorance that surrounds them. There are several courses open, but none so direct as that offered by the Press Council to newspaper readers. To begin with, the teacher should get hold of a copy of *The British Code of Advertising Practice* available from the Advertising Association. This is a fair code, on the whole, and if pupils can see that an advertisement breaks it, then their case will be much stronger. The next step is to write to one of the numerous copy committees which would have had direct responsibility for accepting the advertisement. Thus if it appeared in the press, one could write to the Newspaper Society (the addresses of this and other copy committees are to be found in a pamphlet *How Advertising Disciplines Itself* available from the Advertising Association). Advertisements are always guaranteed by the mass media in which they appear, and the pupil can be sure of a courteous response, even though his complaint will probably be rejected.

A further step is to take the matter up with the Advertisement

Investigation Department of the Advertising Association. Once again, this department will acknowledge all correspondence it receives, and it is a powerful agent in the advertising world. Since it never issues a report, however, it is difficult to ascertain the volume or the effect of its work.

There is also a quasi-public body one of whose duties is to deal with complaints from the public. In July 1962 the Advertising Standards Authority was established under the presidency of Sir Arnold Plant, with a board of independent and advertising representatives. Its published aim was 'the promotion and enforcement throughout the United Kingdom of the highest standards of advertising in all media'. Another duty, according to its president, is to be final arbiter on matters of public complaint about the quality or veracity of advertisements. In its first report, published in February 1964, and considered by many to be somewhat overdue, the A.S.A. described its method of dealing with complaints about advertisements. Preferring to work within the existing machinery, the authority would submit all sufficiently documented cases to the British Code of Advertising Practice Committee (CAP committee), a comprehensive organisation established by the Advertising Association itself. The A.S.A. would later consider the committee's ruling, and would reach its final decision, which it would convey both to the CAP committee and to the initiator of the case. The first report stated that the rulings handed down by the authority have been accepted by the constituent advertising organisations, and by well over half of the complainants.

This is reassuring news, but it is impossible to glean from the report much idea of what the complaints were about and whether they were rectified or not. Unlike the Press Council, the A.S.A. prefers to work beyond the public eye, and indeed 'is happy to report that it has not been necessary during this period to resort to publicity as a disciplinary measure to pillory, as it were, a chronic offender against the minimum standards required by the advertising codes'. Thus justice must be done, but not seen to be done. It is true that the report mentions some general rulings it has made over the year, but without chapter and verse. These rulings in themselves, however, make good discussion material for a class.

When the A.S.A. was originally founded, many people felt that its links with the Advertising Association, including an office in the same building, were too close for real independence. Since then, the A.S.A. has shown a certain reticence about its position. Its future reports will therefore be of special interest. Since another important function of the A.S.A. is to suggest modifications of the existing code to the CAP committee, there is no reason why pupils should not send in their own suggestions, as well as any complaints they might have. In both cases, examples of the sort of advertisements referred to should be included.

In all these matters the teacher must be very careful not to act as a prude who ranges himself beyond the class's sympathies. Once more, all that he does with his class will come best through discussion. Even though these discussions do not go as far as he would like, he is performing a valuable service by merely talking about matters which are normally passively accepted, or at least tolerated, rather than openly challenged. That one *can* challenge the world around one, and actually make an impression on it, is something that is utterly new and remarkable to most pupils, and a valuable lesson in itself.

CHAPTER III

FILMS

'There is nothing to compare with the cinema in its impact on human minds and hearts and in the breadth of audience it reaches among the people. The cinema is accessible to all walks of society, to all ages, one may say, from the schoolboy to the aged.' I am sure Mr Khrushchev, who once said this in one of his major speeches, is quite right. The cinema has always been an immensely powerful agent, and when he adds 'It is the most important vehicle for educating the people in the spirit of communism' he is following not only Lenin but also Goebbels in realising the valuable support a one-party state can draw from its own film world. In fact, films can work directly on the emotions in a more powerful way than any other media, and a propagandist who intends to reach and move a vast audience would be wise to select the screen rather than the printed page to get the maximum effect.

But the teacher should not feel absolved from analysing the meaning and message of a film when it cannot be labelled with the views of a major political party. Films made in all countries and conditions are often propaganda for something, although sometimes the intention is not immediately clear. This sort of propaganda can amount to a view of life; it may be noble and it may be almost completely degrading. Once again it is a question of values, and there is an opportunity for the teacher to help and guide.

Is it still worth it? Cinema attendances in this country now (1966) average about $5\frac{1}{2}$ million per week compared with 30 million in 1946. This might seem evidence of a complete decline, and some teachers may feel that television has now completely taken over from the cinema film as a mass medium, and that the teacher need no longer attend to it. Yet 4 million of these 5½ million people are between the ages of 16 and 34, and it is evident that the cinema still has a social function. It is a place to go to to get away from the family, who as likely as not will be grouped around the television set. There will long be a considerable cinema audience of people who have just left school or who are about to do so.

Nor is it enough for the teacher to concentrate on television and to trust that what he says about that medium will also apply to films. There are vital differences: films are much more ambitious in technical and aesthetic matters like editing, lighting and sets, while the themes they can deal with are not limited by the four walls of a television studio and a tiny screen. The film camera can go anywhere; with an 'X' certificate, films can deal with certain topics in the knowledge that there will be no very young people in the audience (although many children under 16 are allowed in to these films, and an 'X' certificate often means a drop in the average age of the audience!). The fact that an audience pays money and sees a film in darkness means that the director can count on a reservoir of attention and concentration; his work is not split by commercials, it can last up to four hours, and he can use colour.

Nevertheless, the future of the cinema is uncertain. At the moment it is still a mass medium, but there have been suggestions recently that it may split into two categories: 'art-house' films for the intelligentsia; and 'pop' films for the rest at their local Odeon or Gaumont. This would be a disaster, for—unlike modern art, music, painting, sculpture, and poetry—the film still draws much of its strength from being a truly popular medium; some of the best films produced have also been box-office hits.

Screen education is now compulsory in Sweden, and in Britain some local authorities will help schools that wish to start work in this field. Many schools already have their own projectors, and films and film extracts can be hired at no great cost; for teachers in the London area, some film extracts are available free of charge. Thus the obstacle to these lessons is generally the teacher himself, who may have the same objection to film in the school as he has to television. Perhaps he would change his mind if he saw the enthusiasm of children for these lessons, since for many pupils the screen is a far more accessible medium than the printed word. No one would want to take literary appreciation out of the time-table; but it seems reasonable to allow it to co-exist with appreciation work done with this universal twentieth-century medium. Film work does not lend itself to the academic streaming commonly found in British schools: everyone sees films and feels free to comment on them. Norman Fruchter, who taught a class of adolescent girls at a day-release college in London, has described the point of a screen education course in these words: 'What such a course can do is to establish the principle that films can be talked about. It can establish the validity of anyone's response, and begin to examine how the film worked to evoke it. The class can become a place where different ways of seeing are examined; and if each boy or girl learns to articulate his perceptions, then more complex and varied responses become possible. The realisation that there are many different ways of responding to a film, and that response involves choice, is probably where the film course ends.'[1] All this is true of literature; but the physical eye and ear are more immediate and powerful than the mind's eye and ear. Work on films can therefore be used as a prelude to critical work generally.

TEACHING FILM TECHNIQUE

Technique is a means to an end, and for this reason the teacher should never teach it in isolation. No one wants to produce the state of mind where pupils notice the continuity errors in *Bicycle Thieves* but not the humanity. For the teacher coming from the outside, it is often a temptation to use technical jargon, which has all the excitement of a new language. But we are teaching children, not subjects, and it is a mistake to let a class

[1] 'Two hours a week', *Sight and Sound,* autumn 1962.

hide the true meaning of a film from itself by irrelevant discussion of 'wipes', 'jump-cuts' and 'dunning'. On the other
hand, a minimum of technical knowledge is desirable if pupils
are going to talk about films in any detail. What is needed is a
vocabulary, to describe not only how a film is made, but why it
has been made in that particular manner, and what this means
to us.

One way of handling these lessons is to work from literature
to film, using a given work of literature as a script and asking
the class how it would appear were it made into a film. Thus
pupils can compare literary technique with film technique, and
an understanding of one will spread to the other. I have found
that the plays of Shakespeare are extremely useful for this: his
plays seem to me to have as much relevance to the film today as
to the stage, and the use of his plays for this purpose has obvious
benefits for the teacher of English. I have described these ideas
elsewhere,[1] but will recapitulate some of them here, using
Julius Caesar for most of my examples.

Shakespeare often has passages of stichomythia where single
lines of dialogue follow rapidly on each other, as in the handkerchief scene of *Othello*, in order to maintain a sudden tension.
Afterwards he will slacken the pace to provide a contrast; the
handkerchief scene ends with Desdemona's longer and sadly
bewildered speeches. This technique is exactly similar to that of
a film editor, who will cut quickly from one thing to another in
moments of excitement but will slow down when he is building
a normal picture. Shakespeare often has a multitude of tiny
scenes, so that in *Antony and Cleopatra*, which has fifteen scenes
in what we now call Act Four, he can give us both sides of the
battle and the activities of its protagonists almost at the same
time. This technique in films is known as 'cross-cutting', and
we often see it in cowboy films: one minute the redskins are
closing in on the coach, the next minute we see the cavalry
galloping along, then we are back with the redskins, oblivious
of their approach, and so on. It is of course a device for showing

[1] 'Shakespeare and Film Technique', *The Use of English*, winter 1962.

two parallel actions at the same time (D. W. Griffith in *Intolerance* used it to show *four* actions at the same time).

When a film editor wishes to imply that time has passed he will fade out a scene, either by fading to black or by superimposing the beginning of the second sequence on the end of the first one. Occasionally he will keep the background constant and fade out the actor, so that we might see a village in summer fade to the same scene in winter, but without the hero, or he may keep the actor constant and fade out the background, so that the star who has just been leaving New York will now reappear in Paris. When Shakespeare wished to imply that a long period of time had passed, he used a chorus; to suggest a short period he probably left the stage empty for a moment. He also used a type of superimposition: Caesar leads Brutus off stage for a taste of wine, and perhaps even before they have quite left the stage Artemidorus enters reading aloud, 'Caesar beware of Brutus'. A last trick played with time in the cinema is the flashback, where we are allowed to see some past experience remembered by one of the characters on the screen.

Ronald Watkins[1] has already pointed out how Shakespeare achieved a similar effect when he recreated past actions and events, which would be difficult to stage, in words so vivid that we can almost see what they are describing. Here is Cassius describing to Brutus how he once saved Caesar's life:

> For once, upon a raw and gusty day,
> The troubled Tiber chafing with her shores,
> Caesar said to me 'Darest thou, Cassius, now
> Leap in with me into this angry flood,
> And swim to yonder point?' Upon the word,
> Accoutred as I was, I plunged in
> And bade him follow: So indeed he did.
>
> The torrent roared, and we did buffet it
> With lusty sinews, throwing it aside
> And stemming it with hearts of controversy;
> But ere we could arrive the point proposed,
> Caesar cried 'Help me, Cassius, or I sink!'

In the same speech, there is another equally striking flashback.

[1] *Moonlight at the Globe* (Michael Joseph).

The angle from which the camera pictures a character is also important. We talk about 'looking up to people' or 'looking down on them', and the camera can do just this with the same effect. Taking someone from a low angle makes them look powerful and menacing, while filming them from above belittles their stature so that they seem insignificant. Cassius does *both* these things to Caesar, as the mood suits him. First he pictures him from a low angle, in order to galvanise Brutus into action:

> Why man, he doth bestride the narrow world
> Like a Colossus, and we petty men
> Walk under his huge legs and peep about
> To find ourselves dishonoured graves.

But he has already belittled Caesar, just before this speech:

> He had a fever when he was in Spain,
> And when the fit was on him, I did mark
> How he did shake: 'tis true this god did shake;
> His coward lips did from their colour fly.

As well as the angle, we must also consider the distance of the camera from its subject, and the artistic reason for this. The close-up gives us a greater insight into personal reactions, while the long shot lets us see a whole scene in perspective. Exactly the same applies to Shakespeare, except that he achieves his effects with words and not with pictures. Thus for a close-up we have the soliloquies, or remarks like:

> The angry spot doth glow on Caesar's brow,
> And all the rest look like a chidden train:
> Calpurnia's cheek is pale, and Cicero
> Looks with such ferret and such fiery eyes
> As we have seen him in the Capitol,
> Being crossed in conference by some senators.

Shakespeare uses a long shot with telling effect in the battle scene, when Pindarus 'ascends a hill' and looking offstage at an imaginary battle tells Cassius that:

> Titinius is enclosed round about
> With horsemen, that make to him on the spur;
> Yet he spurs on. Now they are almost on him.
> Now Titinius! Now some light. O, he lights too.
> He's ta'en.

Pindarus's distance from the action is made tragically clear later on, when it is seen that his information is disastrously wrong.

There are three basic camera movements: side to side (panning); up and down (the tilt); or moving towards or with the actor (tracking). Panning was used unforgettably in the film of *Henry V*, when with Shakespeare's verse, the chorus takes us slowly over the battlefield on the eve of Agincourt. It can also be used to wander over different faces in a crowd, showing individual reactions to a situation, very much as Shakespeare does with his first, second, third and fourth citizens.

The atmosphere created by different sorts of lighting is used to great effect in films and by Shakespeare, although as always he had to make his effect entirely by words. In films lighting is often soft and slightly blurred in emotional or frightening sequences, and sharp in cheerful scenes or at times when the director wishes to emphasise the formal composition of his picture. As Ernest Lindgren pointed out in his *The Art of the Film*, if we see a child in a sick-room and the lighting is soft and dim, we can expect the worst. But if the light is streaming through the window, and the shadows are clear-cut and well defined, a recovery can be expected. Similarly, Shakespeare's lighting is often symptomatic of his characters' feelings; from the first Macbeth complains about the fair and foul weather, and there are constant references in the play to obscurity of vision, just as the idea of moonlight pervades *A Midsummer Night's Dream*.

One of the most striking parallels between the two media can be found by comparing Shakespeare's imagery with the technique of montage in film making. Montage is parallel cutting between an action and its symbolic representation. First made popular by the early Russian directors, it is often used today, particularly by the Indian director Satyajit Ray, who will cut from a scene of a man's death to the sudden picture of a flock of birds flying upwards into the sky. In the cowboy film *Shane*, as the gunman hero unwillingly rides out to do battle the camera periodically cuts back to a shot of three dark and dismal trees, barren and forbidding images. Only the film could attempt to transcribe some of Shakespeare's imagery in this way, when Cleopatra is described as a 'nightingale', 'the day of the world', and Antony is a 'dolphin', and after death a 'fallen star' and a 'withered garland'. Directors who can be called poets of the screen are very rare, but pupils should be made familiar with some of their best work. Since films have now developed the technique of 'deep focus', where both foreground and background can make their effect equally in the same shot, it is no longer necessary to cut from one picture to another to establish a symbolic relationship. Thus in the hands of a good director, the background against which the characters are set will contribute to our emotional reaction. In the films of Michelangelo Antonioni it is important whether we see characters against a barren rocky background, or against sharp and aggressively modern suburban buildings.

Music is used to create atmosphere in Shakespeare's plays: it gives magic to *The Tempest*, suspense to *Othello*, pathos to *King Lear*, an unearthly quality to *A Midsummer Night's Dream*, madness to *Hamlet*, and melancholy to *Julius Caesar* when Lucius plays a 'sleepy tune' to Brutus in his tent. All these uses of music are well-known in the film, and have often been abused, but the parallel is once again very striking. It is also interesting to compare Elizabethan and film conventions. A journey was often shown in the Elizabethan theatre by actors walking around the stage; in films we might see train wheels, or disembarkations. Elizabethan villains were often bastards or deformed; film villains, especially in Westerns, could once be counted on to have a black hat and a small black moustache. Stock characters on the Elizabethan stage included the pathetic child and the bluff soldier; cowboy films often used to have a toothless old campaigner, usually played by Gabby Hayes. There are many other stock characters which the class is sure to think of.

There are still numerous analogies for the teacher to point out. Elizabethan actors soliloquise; films use close-ups and whispered commentaries for the character's private reflections. Most of Shakespeare's comedies have orthodox happy endings—the analogy here immediately presents itself. With Shakespeare, evil gets its deserts, and there is love at first sight—is this still true of films? Do Shakespeare's heroes walk into traps as innocently as many film heroes? Does slapstick in Shakespeare compare with humour in films? Shakespeare's development as a playwright in some way parallels the growth of the film. He begins with melodrama involving a certain amount of overacting, rather as in early films of Griffith or Stroheim. Next his plays become more subtle, but the imagery is still explicit rather than implicit, more simile than metaphor. Eisenstein was the finest director of the silent screen and he too went in for extended comparisons, where the Russian prime minister is ironically compared to Napoleon, or where the dead body of a horse stands for the slaughtered proletariat. Lastly, in Shakespeare's mature period, poetic images are inseparably woven into the meaning of the verse, and emotions are understated rather than underlined. We find something approaching this in the best of the modern cinema, both with the 'deep focus' technique I have described and with the far more subtle approach to feelings and emotions, to be found especially in some of the new French and Italian cinema.

Parallels of this kind enable pupils to picture one medium in terms of another, and in doing so to learn something about both. It is a very 'literary' way of teaching film technique, but for the English teacher it has its uses; it encourages boys and girls not very interested in literature to see it through a medium they know and accept, and, by asking pupils to picture a play in terms of a film, it should give them confidence to think cinematically. If a Shakespeare play is too difficult for a class, another book can be used.

The next stage is to compare an extract from the same story in two different media. The effect of one can be compared with the effect of the other, and the study of technique will be taken one step further, since we read the same material that the film director must have read, and then see what he created on film. For this I have found the opening of *Great Expectations* very useful. On hire as a film extract from the British Film Institute it only lasts two minutes and consists of ten shots, which can obviously be studied in some detail. It shows an extremely brilliant piece of editing by David Lean, and can be seen countless times without boredom. The first shot is of Pip, a small speck on the horizon, running along on a dark stormy day. He passes a gibbet and clambers into a churchyard. There he begins to tear weeds from his parents' grave, when the moaning of the wind causes him to look round in fright. He sees a tree trunk, the bark of which is twisted into what looks like a horrible face. The tree creaks and seems to bend over on to him, he retreats in terror into the arms of the convict, who bends him over backwards and as Pip screams threatens him in a hideous close-up, 'Keep still, you little devil, or I'll cut your throat!'.

Here is the same passage from Dickens:

Ours was the marsh country, down by the river, within, as the river wound, twenty miles of the sea. My first most vivid and broad impression of the identity of things, seems to me to have been gained on a memorable raw afternoon towards evening. At such a time I found out for certain that this bleak place overgrown with nettles was the churchyard; and that Philip Pirrip, late of this parish, and also Georgiana wife of the above, were dead and buried; and that Alexander, Bartholomew, Abraham, Tobias and Roger, infant children of the aforesaid, were also dead and buried; and that the dark flat wilderness beyond the churchyard, intersected with dykes and mounds and gates, with scattered cattle feeding on it, was the marshes; and that the low leaden line beyond was the river; and that the distant savage lair from which the wind was rushing, was the sea; and that the small bundle of shivers growing afraid of it all and beginning to cry, was Pip.

'Hold your noise!' cried a terrible voice, as a man started up from among the graves at the side of the church porch. 'Keep still, you little devil, or I'll cut your throat!'

As a teacher of English as well as film appreciation, one is not concerned with pointing out how the film has followed the book, but rather how each medium achieves its effects in its particular way. The film opens with a brilliant establishing shot, with Pip running against an ominous sky. Dickens describes the same scene as 'a memorable raw afternoon' and the marshes as a 'dark flat wilderness' with the river a 'low leaden line'. Both descriptions create a threatening atmosphere: Dickens through his emotive use of words, Lean through his gloomy setting. Dickens describes the wind as 'rushing' from 'a distant savage lair'; Lean gets the same effect through his use of sound, rightly dispensing with any film music. In the book Pip becomes frightened, 'A small bundle of shivers growing afraid of it all and beginning to cry', while Lean conveys this by a close-up of the boy's face, and by showing us what he saw: the tree and a gravestone that looked like a hunched up body. The pace of Dickens' last extended sentence becomes quicker as we go on, so that we are prepared for something to happen at the end of the paragraph, and the convict's staccato interjection shatters the rhythm of the preceding paragraph. In the film the same effect is achieved as each shot becomes progressively shorter, so that we are unconsciously bracing ourselves for a climax, which is still a shock when it eventually comes.

The class has worked from literature to film, and has compared the two. Lastly, I ask pupils to work from film to literature, and translate film vocabulary back into literary vocabulary. The extract I find particularly useful for this exercise is the last ten minutes of *Bicycle Thieves*, an Italian film directed by Vittorio de Sica in 1949. It is about a very impoverished Italian family, where the father's job depends on his bicycle, which is stolen at the beginning of the film. Eventually he decides to steal one himself, and the extract begins with the father and his nine-year-old son crossing a dark street towards nightfall. Traffic flashes by them, and they stop and sit on the pavement, the father letting his face sink into his hands. From the opposite side of the street comes the noise of a football crowd, and we can see the stadium with a huge sea of bikes parked outside it, guarded by a few policemen. The father paces up and down, and the crowd begins to pour out of the stadium. Suddenly he sees a bike propped up against a doorway down a street. He sends his son home in an abrupt way that raises the boy's suspicions, so that he only makes a half-hearted attempt to get the tram and is turned away. Meanwhile the father runs towards the bike and mounts it. The owner appears, and soon quite a large crowd is following the father and eventually drags him off. As he is led off to the police he is pushed and hit by various people, and it is in this state that his son sees him, and runs towards him crying out 'Papa!'. This softens the heart of the owner who agrees to release the father now that he has been thoroughly humiliated. The son is deeply ashamed of him, and walks at a careful distance, but as he looks up he sees that his father is crying. He reaches up to hold his hand and the film ends as they are swallowed up in the crowd.

Pupils are always very moved by this film, and can remember it in great detail. I ask them to write down the story, from the point of view of the father or of the son. Little of the film's technique escapes a pupil who is really interested: the snatches of music summing up the father's temptation, or the boy's horror on seeing his father for the second time. Angled camera shots tell us how the son and the father see each other, and we can see the lines of hunger and fatigue on the older man's face. All this is written down using words instead of sound and images, and by doing this I hope to teach not just the 'how' of cinema technique, but also the 'why'. This knowledge can be brought into English lessons in many other ways, and when pupils are writing a story I often criticise it in film language. Thus if the story begins too abruptly, I remind them that we need an establishing shot to tell us where we are. If a pupil describes someone as having a 'nice' face, I ask him to focus his camera better, to give us a more accurate idea; or if it is a description of a set scene, I ask him to swing his camera around to bring in as much as he can. There is a considerable body of common critical language between the two media, which is not surprising since we often see events unfolding in our mind's eye when we read a novel, which is nothing less than our private cinema screen where we 'project film' of what we are imagining.

There are many other questions pupils should ask themselves about a film when they are seeing it. Is there real tension in the film, or is it merely achieved by quick editing rhythms and the right sort of music? Does the background play an important part, or could the action have happened almost anywhere else with exactly the same effect? Does the music add another dimension to the film, by enabling us to know people's thoughts and emotions, and by letting us gauge mood or atmosphere, or does it merely hurry along our emotions? Does the camera treat us honestly, or does it attempt to trick us by too many angle shots, speeded-up movement (as in many fights and chases) or even slow motion (often used when people fall in films)? Are the characters on the screen really convincing, or are they obviously acting a part? Does the sound track add anything to the film, or is it just a background? In fact, the sound track of a film is just as selective as the picture we see, since it is nearly always recorded afterwards, when the shooting is safely over. Thus dialogue is post-synchronised, and so are songs. This enables the singer to smile charmingly when she sings on the screen, but to pull all the strange faces many singers find essential to produce a good note in the privacy of the recording studio. There is a library of sound, which can dub in anything from angry crowds to horses' hooves; there is also a 'footstep' girl who will dub in any footsteps required with perfect accuracy. If pupils do not see the reason for post-dubbed sound, they should try recording into a tape-recorder, where they will realise the problem of extraneous noise, which is obviously far worse in a film studio. Paradoxically, natural sound when recorded often seems curiously unreal, so the artificial sound, as well as being much easier to record, can seem much better than the real thing. Pupils should try recording water lapping (slopping water in a half-filled paint tin) or eggs frying (crinkling cellophane).

Another way of teaching film technique is to take classes through the history of the cinema, letting them see how each technique originated and what has become of it since. This obviously would not do for a complete course, since no one wants to look at all films merely from the point of view of their place in history, but some film history can be most interesting, and children of most ages enjoy making the toys that began the movement. These can be seen at the Science Museum in London, and at least two of them can be made in the classroom. (More of them can be seen in the 1963 edition of *Screen Education Year Book*.) The thaumotrope is a card with a different picture on each side, so that, for example, if it is rotated quickly by string threaded at each end, the bird on one side will go into the cage on the other. Pupils can also make their own flip books, which work like a cartoon film, in that each drawing differs a little from the one before; when the pages of drawings are flipped through together, they give the impression of continuous movement.

There are many extracts available from the British Film Institute showing the growth of technique in the film. We can see the work of the Lumière brothers, who brought us our first moving picture, and Méliès who gave us the first story. *The Great Train Robbery* was the first 'chase' film, and shows the first example of panning and cross-cutting. D. W. Griffith gave us the close-up and long shot, and Eisenstein produced the first example of dynamic editing; in the Odessa steps sequence from *Battleship Potemkin*, there are no less than 160 separate shots in only six minutes of film. *Kameradschaft* directed by G. W. Pabst shows the first really imaginative use of sound, and Orson Welles' *Citizen Kane* invented the technique of deep focus. These are merely the high points of a continuing growth, and the teacher can end his summary by describing some of the developments of today: cinerama, 3-D, and even smellovision. (Ezra Goodman recalls a poster advertising this last technique: 'First they moved (1893), then they talked (1927), now they smell (1959)!') The teacher should not neglect the silent screen. Some of its directors reached an understanding of the power of the visual image that has never been equalled since. Although silent films tend to lend themselves to historical analysis, there is a great deal that can be learnt from them, which pupils would never by themselves have found out, since silent films are usually made ridiculous on the contemporary screen by being shown at the wrong speed.

Nevertheless, modern films are what really concern the teacher, because these are what his pupils normally see. Before he passes on to discuss them, perhaps he should outline briefly the production process, so that the credit titles flashed at a cinema audience will have more significance. In many ways the pattern resembles that found in television. The producer puts up the money, and the production company takes ultimate responsibility. The director is in charge of the eventual appearance of the film, together with the editor. When the film is finally made, it must find a distributor (or renter) who will publicise it and find it exhibitors, or in other words cinemas willing to show the film. Thus few producers will dare make films that will not please Wardour Street—the distributing centre. The Rank organisation, which owns the Odeon and Gaumont-British circuit, and the Associated British Cinema circuit (A.B.C.) in which Warner Brothers have a 37 per cent interest, have solved the problem for themselves by becoming their own distributors and exhibitors, by owning the individual cinemas, 710 between them, and the distributing rights in their own films. Rank also has an agreement with Columbia, Universal, United Artists, Walt Disney and Twentieth Century Fox film companies to accept a certain number of the films they produce, while A.B.C. has a similar arrangement with Anglo-Amalgamated, Warner-Pathe, Paramount and Metro-Goldwyn-Mayer film companies. Most of these agreements involve 'conditional selling', which means that films will be accepted whether they are known to be good or bad. Although films made or contracted to Rank and A.B.C. can always be sure of a cinema, independent producers have no such assurance since there is no 'blanket' agreement by the two networks to accept any of their films. Instead each independent film is judged according to its merits and the conventional pattern of the films normally exhibited by the two networks. Unless independent producers can use these circuits, their films will not be seen by many people, since there are very few profitable independent cinemas. Perhaps this is why there have been few controversial films made in this country, since there are too few distributors willing to give them a showing. Recently there have been slightly more daring policies about films, and the class would do well to see whether there is any 'product pattern' in the films put forward by any one company in the current year and to note the distributors who seem to be interested in better types of film.

DISCUSSING FILM

It is important for the teacher to establish the point that films *matter*. As in the case of television, pupils should bring to the school anything that is relevant, whether it be photographs of film stars, 'show-biz' gossip, or film posters. The teacher may be able to get a local cinema manager to lend him some old 'stills' (pictures used to advertise a film) or other publicity material.[1] This collection can be arranged in an eye-catching way on the classroom wall. Another permanent exhibition can be designed to draw pupils' attention to good films on current release. The local press is not very helpful here, often merely reproducing the hand-outs sent by the distributor's publicity department, so the teacher should collect criticisms from the national press and exhibit them with the name of the film. He should also have a stop-press column, where a pupil might see a film on its first day and write a review for the rest of the class.

However, many pupils will not see these films, and the teacher cannot afford to base his lessons on films which only half his class has seen. Instead he must bring the film into the classroom, by showing films and extracts which he can easily hire. The use of extracts is controversial; some teachers maintain that it is quite wrong to take a piece of film out of its context and put it up for full analysis, but often the teacher has no alternative. A ten-minute extract will fit well into a normal school period, whereas a whole film would be difficult—and very expensive—to handle. But extracts must be chosen with

[1] Some generous film companies will also send 'stills' of their films to schools at request.

care, since no class likes being left in mid-air, and will not feel disposed to talk about a film if all it can think of is 'What happened next?' Thus extracts of the last few moments of a film often make the best material, since no one feels let down, and also it is here that the director often makes a personal summing-up of what the plot and the action meant for him. Extracts are also useful for showing the badness of some films. No teacher would want his class to sit through an hour of rubbish, but ten minutes or so is quite long enough to make many points without showing more of the film than one would wish. This argument also applies to thoroughly bad films that may have one brilliant scene, like the earthquake scene in *San Francisco*, or the locusts' raid in *The Good Earth*. With good material the extract offers a marvellous chance to analyse in depth. It should of course be seen twice, or even three times. The teacher can fill in the story, and each showing will reveal to a class more of the skill and meaning in the pictures in front of it. How the teacher conducts these lessons is for him to decide. One useful way is to show each extract once, have a discussion of what the pupils have actually seen, then show it again, now that they know the story, to analyse how it is treated. If there are still more points of interpretation to be brought out, it can be seen a third time, without the sound track if the teacher is concerned to make a point conveyed by the visual aspect alone.

One guide to the teacher in his choice of extracts is that he should choose films illustrating particular genres. Each week will bring a general discussion on the quality of the film, plus the special questions of content and interpretation raised by particular types of film. Many of the questions asked will be the same as those put during the lessons about television, with the difference that we have the material actually in front of us.

It is good tactics for the teacher to begin with an extract from a Western, since he will come up against lively interest and a strong body of information. Nevertheless, every class is surprised when it hears about the tricks used in the average cowboy film, and although one does not want to destroy too many illusions, there is no harm in mildly debunking the bad mass-produced film. So the class hears that one of the last cowboy actors to ride his own horse with any confidence was Tom Mix, and since then extras have performed most of those daring feats that so excite a cinema audience. When we see the hero in close-up on a galloping horse, it is the scenery that is moving, and the horse may be an electrically driven model. Pupils never believe this immediately, and unfortunately the extract that best shows it, *When the Daltons Rode*, has been withdrawn from the British Film Institute Library. The signs of an electrically driven horse are a fixed expression, glassy and unblinking eyes, and, if the art director is not careful, a just-visible row of metal studs joining its two halves in the middle. When we see a close-up of a coach careering along, again it is the scenery that is rushing past, while the coach is being rocked by hand, and a fan is blowing the actor's hair about. If the camera pulls away from this shot, and we actually see a coach in real flight, it is interesting to look at the foreground, where the tracks of the camera car taking the film are often clearly visible. When bullets are fired they are accompanied from the gun barrel by a cloud of chalk, while horses will fall on their side, not neck and crop as in the Grand National, since there is often a rein attached to their forelegs which when pulled topples the horse over and enables the rider to roll away safely. Killing in cowboy films, as befits the accuracy with which revolvers can hit any object (except the horse, which never seems to get wounded), is unreal and stylised. A B.F.I. film, *Critic and 3.10 to Yuma*, contains a very interesting discussion by John Freeman of the appeal of cowboy films, and an extract from *Stagecoach*, directed by John Ford, also illustrates many of the clichés and tricks I have already mentioned, and has fully stylised music; if one played the sound track alone, one would know exactly when the Indians made their first appearance, and exactly when the cavalry make their last-minute rescue.

Pupils also enjoy reading about the West, which can be

another good way for them to see cowboy films in perspective. In *The Film Teacher's Handbook, 1959,* Charles Cain gives a very useful book-list, and some good questions that pupils might try to answer: 'What was the Wild West really like? Was Jesse James the romantic hero the cinema often shows him to be? Was Calamity Jane really a glamorous cowgirl? Did the gun-fight at the OK Corral actually take place? Was the American Indian merely a murderous savage, or did he often have good reason to attack the white man? Was Doc Holliday a real person? In how many gun duels was Wyatt Earp involved?'

The world of the gangster, though equally popular, could hardly be more different. Instead of the wide open spaces he works in speakeasies in Chicago. The cowboy dresses simply and is often shy about women; the gangster's clothes are expensive and he has a loud taste in girl friends. The cowboy hero believes in chivalry, and his pleasures are simple; the gangster is worldly, loves money, and will shoot a man in the back if necessary. Of course he is not the hero of the film in the same sense as the cowboy is, or as Humphrey Bogart was before the war, but he can have a huge and devoted following. He often behaves with the proverbial honour amongst thieves, and never complains when he is caught. He is tough, and, although the last ten minutes of the film will remind us that crime does not pay, usually does quite well until his downfall, which is usually caused by a casual oversight.

Nowadays the gangster has been largely replaced as the focal point in crime films by the tough F.B.I. man, who may behave in a way remarkably like that of many gangsters. The mood of the film is the same. The opening shots may be of Los Angeles, with strident music and a fast montage of file cards, finger prints, and crime-detecting machines while the voice of an announcer will remind us of the many crimes committed by the underworld each year. Soon the music will hush, and the camera will focus on one of the main scenes, and yet another story begins. Many of these films are made extremely cheaply: indeed, a whole series may be shot in a few days. Sets are few, and the camera tends to be static. There are many long close-ups, and frequent cuts from one face to another, easily the cheapest as well as one of the most tedious ways of making a film. Interest is maintained by the endless process of cross-examination as a form of dialogue between the detective and the various suspects. Another popular way of passing the time in this sort of film is to include trial scenes, all with full legal circumlocution.

At its best the screen criminal world is full of overtones and undercurrents where nothing is quite what it seems. Perhaps this is the fascination of the crime film, and it is shown well in a B.F.I. extract from *The Maltese Falcon*, which introduces us to a world where nothing can be taken for granted. Even the camera is tilted, and violence is sudden and unexpected. At a more sophisticated level, an extract from *The Third Man*, available from Rank Films, shows us very much the same thing, this time with the aid of insinuating music. People have always loved mysteries, and will sit through most films that begin with a seemingly unaccountable crime, with such familiar lines as: 'Do you mean to say that the man locked the door from the inside after he shot himself?' The teacher can concentrate on this fascination, and can discuss with his class the changing role of the detective, what we really feel about the crook, and whether the film would have had a dangerous effect if it showed that crime *did* pay.

There are some war films which treat war as if it were fun, with John Wayne missing death by inches and behaving as if he were bronco-busting, with the Japanese navy as horses. We see violence but not its effects, and it therefore has little emotional impact. This sort of film has prolonged 'joking relationships' between the sergeant and his men, and if it is an English film it is full of regional types: the Scotsman, the Welshman and the Irishman, not to mention the Londoner whose Cockney humour conceals a heart of gold. The officer, however, will be a toff, and in most of these films social barriers will be as firm as ever they have been; each man will know not only his place, but his rank as well.

There is always a battle in the last reel, and a few deaths, but in general this sort of war is an opportunity for community singing and facile camaraderie. A variation of this type is the film that treats war as heroic, where one side is evil, and it is the duty of the other side to purge the earth of these monsters. There is less fun here, and more tight-lipped heroism. Violence is treated realistically, but since we have no sympathy for the other side we are inclined not to worry about what happens to them, and there is little analysis of what causes war, or what the soldiers think they are fighting for. A good example of this can be found in the extract from *Alexander Nevsky*, directed by Eisenstein and distributed by Contemporary Films.

The other sort of war film is more honest, and presents war very much as seen by the soldier poets of the First World War. Here, human beings on one side are fighting recognisable human beings on the other. The real enemy is seen to be not one army or the other, but war, and the people and emotions that make it possible. Neither violence nor its effects are played down, and we see not only what their side does to us, but also what our side does to them. The extract from *Children of Hiroshima*, showing the explosion of the atomic bomb, is a most telling example of this, and still tragically topical.

The B.F.I. has some rare propaganda films; and though it is no longer seen in the cinema in its most blatant forms, pupils should learn something about this technique of mass persuasion. There is a horrifying puppet film made in Germany before the Second World War for the benefit of primary school children, called *The Boy Who Wanted to Know What Fear Was*. We see a young boy going to a castle, and being beset by the most terrifying phantoms, which he disposes of by methods horribly prophetic of the concentration camps: one phantom he beheads, another he thrusts into a furnace; to pass the time he takes a skull and, with the help of a lathe, turns it into a ball with which he plays skittles, using human bones for pegs. The film's intentions are obvious: to break down traditional feelings about death, turning it into a matter for self-confident joking and callousness. Another of the B.F.I.'s propaganda films is *Britain Can Take It*, fairly restrained and understated in tone even though it was made in 1940. 'Here they come', says the commentator in a voice heavy with weary resignation, and in a moment we see bombs exploding everywhere over London. There is, of course, no panic, and the mood, though modest, is nevertheless defiant. 'German bombers are creatures of night', says the commentator, 'And very soon they will scurry back to safety'. This makes an interesting comparison with what he says about R.A.F. bombers, 'soon to fly deep into the heart of Germany'. A German newsreel, also on hire, makes similar points in favour of its own side. The musical accompaniment grows very sombre, and the announcer lowers his voice to a shocked hush as we see damage caused by British bombs on Normandy villages.

Horror films are very popular with adolescent pupils, not least since many of the children are not legally allowed to see them. These films are a way in which adolescents test themselves: the louder they laugh, the more grown-up they feel. Crude ones make their effect with shock tactics, using revolting close-ups of mutilation or of disembodied brains in clinical detail. The teacher can point out that this is not the only way of creating this effect, and that it is better and more subtle to suggest things than to state them baldly. In fact these films are almost invariably bad, with titles as ridiculous as their plots: *I was a teenage Were-Wolf* is a good example. The B.F.I. have an extract from *The Cabinet of Dr Caligari*, which, although over forty years old, still has a marvellous power to evoke a strange and mysterious atmosphere. Two extracts from *The Wages of Fear* create more suspense than any monster in the crypt or hunchback in the belfry. The film concerns two lorries carrying a load of nitro-glycerine, which will explode at the slightest jolt. The characters in the film seem very real, and the film creates suspense in the classic manner: close-ups become larger and larger, sounds become louder and more significant. At the end of one highly tense episode the men relieve their feelings in a way unusual in films but highly delightful for any class; these extracts are always extremely popular. This film was the first foreign language subtitled film to receive a national distribution in Britain. It is itself a useful way to break down any resistance pupils might have to foreign films, though this has also been done by the B.B.C.'s excellent series 'International Film Season'.

There are many documentary films on hire: the B.F.I. have a composite reel, *Film and Reality,* which illustrates the documentary's many different styles. One extract from Eisenstein's *The General Line* illustrates the lyrical documentary, made up from edited shots of people and objects put into close apposition. This can be compared with an extract from Edgar Anstey's *Housing Problems,* a severely factual documentary about slums; though this was made in 1936 it uses exactly the same technique as television interviewing today. A documentary film that pupils always appreciate is Richard Massingham's *Introducing the New Worker* (Central Film Library) which shows the right and the wrong way for the first day at work to go, and always gets a good response. Documentaries made by the National Film Board of Canada are always of a very high standard: *Lonely Boy,* the study of a pop singer, is the best study ever made of singers and their effect on teenagers.

From 'straight' films that do not fall into any obvious category we should get an idea of the differences between people and the complexities of their relationships to each other and to their environment. A film of particular use to teachers is *Twelve Angry Men,* and the B.F.I. have a shortened version, *Critic and Twelve Angry Men.* The story concerns a jury who have to consider a murder charge. Ingeniously, the director explores each character. Soon we feel that we are personally acquainted with them, and this gives the teacher a great opportunity to explore character, motivation, emotion, and reason in human affairs. The fact that the film was made cheaply, is set almost entirely in one room, and was a box-office disaster is also something to talk about.

Hollywood sometimes used to make films about current social problems, such as the colour bar, antisemitism, and unmarried mothers. It is important that such films should be good, and that they should explore their problems honestly, and not merely exploit their sensational aspects (one is reminded of a film about unmarried mothers where the distributors suggested a mother-and-baby show and a competition for the best short story on 'My First Love' as the film's local publicity). Nor should the film over-simplify matters: as one writer said, most films may show antisemitism, but they will never show semitism. Obviously the test of real tolerance is not whether we can put up with a minority seen to be noble and misunderstood, but whether we can live with minorities which may have all our own failings. As Penelope Houston writes: 'The dialogue can be as high-minded as it pleases, and the audience can take it in its stride, for toleration of an Alec Guinness or a Gregory Peck implies no strain'.[1]

Adolescents can perhaps judge the issue more clearly when it comes to problem films made about themselves, the teenagers.

Teenagers tend to have a strangely dual image in many films: either they are 'angels with dirty faces', or else they go in for theft, rape, or even murder, and never ride a motor-bike for any but aggressive reasons. Schools in films are seldom truly pictured, and a study of how different films have distorted them would be most instructive. Many of the current complaints one can hear about schools and teenagers seem based more on film images and press horror stories than on any recognisable reality. An extract available from Rank Films' *Violent Playground* shows Stanley Baker battling with local roughs. The sequence ends with a frightening jive, where the youngsters weave in and out, making weird hysterical movements to a jazz record. This can be compared with another film about adolescents: *We are the Lambeth Boys*, distributed by Ford. Here we can see them as bright interesting people with a perfectly healthy desire to dance, which they do twice in long

[1] *The Contemporary Cinema.*

sequence. Which film gives the more accurate picture? Do either or both of the films exaggerate in one way or another? There will be no difficulty in getting a class to discuss this sort of issue.

Period films often try to compensate for their essential unreality by emphasising costumes, sets and enormously complex spectacular scenes. The stories of these epics are often strangely lifeless, as if overshadowed by all the action going on around them. The language used tends to be an odd amalgam of ancient and modern, and many of the spoken lines remind one of Max Beerbohm's parody of a historical play:

> 'Leonardo, have you seen Michelangelo?'
> 'Sure, I passed him on the Rialto with Benvenuto.'

The B.F.I., however, have extracts from films that cannot be described as 'epic', but manage to convey a real impression of the past. In an extract from a French film, *Monsieur Vincent*, we see the priest arriving at a village. All the doors are closed, and there is an unearthly silence. As he moves down the street, a shower of stones cascades around him from one or two unseen assailants. He enters the church to find it full of farmyard animals. Eventually he meets a broken-down old woman who tells him the mystery of the village: that the plague has broken out. The film offers a splendid chance to make the class feel the reality of another age, and it is also an example of the scenario telling the story: hardly a word is said in the extract, but the mood becomes progressively more sinister and forbidding. An extract from *Oliver Twist* (Rank Films) shows Oliver meeting the Dodger in the middle of London, with pigs and chickens running around in a market being held near St Paul's. The two make a journey through some grimy slums to meet Fagin. The setting is convincing, and makes an interesting comparison with the book.

The musical is one of the cinema's most distinctive forms. It can of course play safe, and give us a naturalistic setting from which the star will occasionally emerge to sing to us, accompanied by an invisible orchestra in the background. Another type of musical is about the 'Big Show', and its final number is a huge spectacle which could just as easily be seen on the stage. The most inventive musical is the sort that uses all the resources of the camera, art-director and lighting crew. An extract from *An American in Paris* (B.F.I.) gives the class an idea of the possibilities. The abstract settings and lengthy ballet sequences might not be to many pupils' taste, but will help them realise that musicals do not have to be static and uninventive. It is at any rate a frank form of fantasy; can the class think of other films that are also fantasy, but which pretend to be realistic?

Comedy styles have changed completely since the early slapstick films, but many of these films are still commercially viable today. There are many good extracts available from the B.F.I.: for example, Chaplin's *Easy Street*, Harry Langdon's *Long Pants*, or Laurel and Hardy's *Musical Box*. Each comedian has his individual style; Chaplin relies heavily on mime and individual gags, where we can see the skills he must have learned in the music hall. Like other comedians, he will use a joke to its utmost—a process known as 'milking'—and will then suddenly bring about a surprise twist ('topping' a gag). There is an element of suppressed fear in his humour; he nearly always just escapes from some frightful encounter with the huge man who so often turns up. He is of course very critical of social conditions in his films: in *Easy Street* he shows the poverty of the slums, and himself feeds the many children as if they were chickens. Harry Langdon is a different sort of clown, very much in the Buster Keaton tradition; he wanders through his films blank-faced and unsmiling, missing disaster by inches without ever knowing it. This is the style of Stan Laurel in the Laurel and Hardy series, in contrast to the more practical but irascible personality of Oliver Hardy. Most of their humour is slapstick, but marvellously subtle in its timing. They will fall through roofs and crash through doors, and by insisting on their right to retaliate if they are insulted, can completely wreck a car or a house in a matter of minutes. They can get almost any amount of humour out of one situation, and remain two of the

93

great artists of the silent screen. Unlike others, they were able
to cope with the new challenge of sound, which tended to desert
slapstick and make humour far more verbal. There are some
modern artists like Jacques Tati whose humour is still mainly
visual and can be seen in an extract from *Jour de Fête* (B.F.I.).
More typical of today, but many would say not so funny, is the
sort of verbal humour found in the Sergeant Bilko series,
examined in a short film *You'll Never Get Rich* (B.F.I.). These
films have drifted away from the eternal comic characters: the
fat man and the little man, or the simple innocent. Instead, the
comic has become slicker, and his humour has tended to become
less pointed. Many of his films have a very predictable and
unfunny sentimental story line co-existing uneasily with the
comic relief. With occasional exceptions, these films would
never dream of attacking any of our more powerful institutions
in the way that Chaplin did. Instead, they tend to turn their
humour on some of society's scapegoats: the bearded artist,
or the blue-stocking intellectual.

The cartoon is a poor relation to the comic film, and much of
its humour is harsh and brutal by comparison. The B.F.I. has a
useful composite film, *Drawings That Walk and Talk*, which gives
extracts from cartoons ranging from Felix to Popeye. Although
no one suggests that these should be taken too seriously, it is
remarkable how much of the humour is concerned with cruelty,
or even sadism. In this film we see a skeleton dance (quite
terrifying for smaller children), Mickey Mouse swinging a cat
by the tail and torturing other animals, and Popeye stamping
hard on an enemy's hand. Perhaps we find these things funny
and permissible because cartoon figures and not real people are
doing them, but the question remains: why do we find them
funny at all?

The last category I would deal with, and perhaps the most
fascinating, consists of English films made about England.
Unlike cowboy films, these films are about something we have
first-hand knowledge of, and they offer the class an excellent
opportunity for informed criticism and appreciation. Before the

war, these films used to be about people and a country that hardly existed. Its houses would consist of huge rooms with French windows and a gleaming lawn, and there would be a full quota of domestic servants. They would be set in the country; we saw little of industrial Britain, presumably because it was too close to reality. Some of the male characters would speak in an extraordinary sort of schoolboy slang, to which the heroines would reply in impeccable Knightsbridge accents. The plot might be frivolous, to do perhaps with ghosts or comic criminals, or it might take a more serious turn, and using the acting resources of the West End theatre, give us something approaching melodrama. Real problems tended to be shirked, as in *Shipyard Sally* where Gracie Fields won orders for the unemployed Clyde ship-workers by virtue of her fine singing, or *South Riding*, starring Ralph Richardson, about municipal corruption. Both films, incidentally, finished optimistically to the loud strains of *Land of Hope and Glory*.

Since the production of *Room at the Top* in 1958 things have changed immensely, and the British cinema, at one time the despair of the international film world, actually began winning prizes at Film Festivals. British films are now much tougher, and centre their action around more realistic characters with recognisable problems. These films have sometimes become monotonous whenever the director's attitude towards the plot and the location has become predictable. There might be too much spirit of 'mass observation', and too little sense of style. Nearly all films of this genre have been based on successful novels, and with them they make good discussion material. Are these characters real? Where do they live, and what is significant about it? Is there a happy ending, or just an ending? Were you bored, and if so, why? Have you read the book, and how does it compare with the film?

Once more it must be emphasised that films of different kinds all share the same basic technique. Thus, when we discuss *Oliver Twist* as an example of a period film, this should not stop us from considering its many other aspects: how do we know Oliver is lonely and bewildered, and in what way does the journey to Fagin's den become more and more frightening? Even if the teacher wishes to conduct each lesson according to plan, the class may often not let him, and he must to a certain extent be led by the direction of the discussion. It is no good beginning by talking about dynamic editing in *Battleship Potemkin*, if the class wants to be satisfied immediately about the fate of the baby in the pram that went rolling down the steps. He must make his point about editing later, when the right context arrives. There is never any shortage of points to be raised in film discussion; the difficulty lies rather in keeping them within reasonable bounds.

CLASSWORK ON FILMS

Following up films after projection can be difficult, since they are appreciated emotionally, and it is hard to get reactions down on paper. Thus the normal way to conduct these lessons is by discussion immediately after the extract has been seen. That can be extended by showing contrasting extracts, or extracts which complement each other. Some of these discussions can be recorded on tape and played to other classes, to start them talking. Pupils who are awkward at expressing themselves on paper can be very active in these discussions, and can remember whole scenes long after they have seen the film. But there are also opportunities for written work, and the pupils should keep a film diary, on the same lines as their television diary (see p. 150). Every film seen should be recorded, with the main details of its production team and of its plot, with the pupil's own criticism coming at the end. If he can find pictures or other published criticism to go with his report, he should include them too. There should also be a film exercise book, where the teacher gives notes to the pupil and where each extract shown is recorded, with any details the teacher thinks necessary. Pupils should also draw in it, and stick in pictures or scraps of film. The book should be as readable and attractive as possible.

Pupils can also express their reactions by writing as if they were a character in the film. Or they can take well-known film conventions and weave a story around them. Elmer Rice has done this in his *Voyage to Purilia*. The hero lands in Purilia, where he finds that the girls never eat or sneeze, and always disappear after marriage. The only mining is gold-mining, otherwise there is very little industry; state governors exist solely to give wronged citizens last-minute reprieves, while negroes are only seen as train porters or jazz musicians; Purilians are moved by music, but find gout and toothache extraordinarily funny; amnesia is often caused by a blow on the head, but is always cured shortly afterwards by another blow; the restaurants are very crowded, but there is always an empty table conveniently near the cabaret. Sophisticated pupils can write essays on the current assumptions of many films. Roger Manvell has made a list of some of these.[1] For example, men are the source of money for women, a sock on the jaw is an honest man's answer, sex is probably the most important sensation in life, brainless patriotism is preferable to national self-criticism, to be foreign is to be under suspicion, and to be Eastern is to be horrific. There is obviously far more to be said about this, and the teacher will discover how much more his pupils know about this sort of detail than he does. At the end of the course there could even be a film exam, so long as it is not allowed to have the deadening effect that exams so often do. In this, I should not test pupils on past work, but show them an extract and ask them to write about various aspects of its technique and content. This is an exam which many pupils actually enjoy doing.

Most popular writing about films is concerned with gossip about film stars. It is of course possible to have good films without stars. The first British film star was a dog, who played *Rescued by Rover* (B.F.I.), and heroines of films were often called after the cinemas in which their films were shown, like the Biograph Girl, who could be seen in the little Biograph Cinema

[1] *Film.*

still standing by Victoria Station. This previously anonymous girl was seized by one of the first 'ballyhooligans', who bought her from Biograph, gave her name to the press and then announced that she was dead. Her triumphant resurrection was one of the first publicity stunts. Since then, the process has grown enormously: women committed suicide on Valentino's death, and Gary Cooper's fan club suggested that he run for president, since he showed such an admirable understanding of democracy in his film *Mr Deeds Goes to Town*. Although the great era of Hollywood film stars is now over, a few stars and popular singers can still command adulation equal to anything in the history of star worship, and the teacher should give some time to analysing and describing this phenomenon. Many of his pupils will have first-hand knowledge of it.

It is impossible to separate the effect of the stars on their public from the effect of their publicity agents, since anything that is real about the star is only incidental to the image that the agent wishes to build. What do people worship: the myth or the reality? Stars' names are often changed from something plain to something fancy, either alliterative, tough-sounding, or seductive. Thus, Norma Jean Baker becomes Marilyn Monroe, and Roy Fitzgerald becomes Rock Hudson, not to mention Sabrina, Dorothy Lamour and Zsa-Zsa Gabor. The whole artificial process has been brilliantly described in Edgar Morin's *The Stars*, and Ezra Goodman's *The Fifty-Year Decline and Fall of Hollywood*. Once it has been decided to launch a star, Morin writes, 'She learns to walk, loses her accent, is taught to sing, to dance, to stand, to sit still, to "hold herself". She is instructed in literature, ideas...her car, her servants, her dogs, her goldfish, her birds, are chosen for her'. So are her hobbies, however elevated they might be. 'There are few philosophical, psychological, political or sociological works that Bob Montgomery has not studied. He is on friendly terms with Hemingway, Noel Coward, and the most brilliant of today's youth. But he can also hold his own with engineers, doctors, and university professors.' There must also be a gimmick, like

Kim Novak's favourite colour, lavender, or her reputedly favourite means of transport, a bicycle; Goodman reports that her fans too will wear lavender bow ties or blouses. The stars' houses are 'pseudo-feudal chateaux, or copied from antique temples, with marble swimming-pools, menageries, and private railroads',[1] or indeed a fur-lined bathroom. The cinemas in which these people have their films shown have names that reflect their semi-regal status: the Coliseum, the Empire the Palace. Has there ever been a cinema with an unassuming name? If pupils are in the habit of reading film gossip, they should be asked to look out for extravagances like these, and perhaps make a list of them.

Stars are naturally beautiful or handsome, yet even this quality is not all it seems. Marilyn Monroe had her hairline plucked, her teeth straightened and cartilage added to her chin before she was thought suitable for public show. Stars often have their favourite lighting expert and camera man who know exactly how to make them look their best. Max Factor and Elizabeth Arden both started in Hollywood, where they became skilful at presenting made-up faces to the world. The height of some film stars is sometimes concealed. Goodman reports a remark from a veteran Hollywood director, Billy Wilder, on Audrey Hepburn: 'Audrey is a tall girl. She is five foot seven, I think she'll need tall leading men. Maybe she'll have to wear flat heels in "Sabrina" and Bogart will have to wear high heels. But if we can do it with Alan Ladd, we can do it with anybody'. It is reported that when Alan Ladd and Sophia Loren had to run along together in one film the lady had to have a special trench dug for her, so that she might not tower over the gentleman. Film stars seldom do the brave things that we see on the screen; for these, extras and stunt men are employed.

All screen stars' marriages are reported to be idyllic until the divorce comes. When they are on the set, the same incident is reported about so many of them, that one is bound to suspect

[1] Morin.

the press agent at work again. Goodman makes a list of some of these: 'The story about the studio gateman who did not recognise an eminent star in costume...the calamity story on how a light fell off a cat walk, narrowly missing the leading man...a search for an unknown to star in a big production (a star usually gets the role)'.[1]

Publicity agents work largely through film or fan magazines, and film columns in newspapers. There are different styles of approach. Sometimes information is merely about 'the dress, diet, and metabolism of film actors'.[1] There is also the 'poor little rich girl' approach, which Goodman calls 'Hollywood heartbreak': 'Why Dwayne Hickman will never marry', where we learn how frightfully lonely and insecure film stars really are. There is always room to mention the film they are about to appear in. Then there is the slightly more salacious approach. 'Hayley Mills' wicked, wicked ways', or 'How Liz and Burton make love, eight pages of pictures'. Only the titles are prurient; the stories turn out to be innocuous pieces on how Miss Mills is 'wild about shoes', and eight pages of stills from *Cleopatra*. Lastly, there is the gossip that is more pointed, and aimed at hurting. 'Dick is in love with French beauty—They plan to marry when her divorce is final. Only trouble is, Dick is making pictures here, and her next two are in France. Can their love survive this long distance?—I wonder.' This is mild compared with the sort of thing printed in *Confidential Magazine*, which dealt only with the worst kind of scandal, backed with 'candid' photographs. There will always be a market for this approach, as long as the other sort of gossip is so flaccid and puerile; but it is a strange reflection on film fans that they enjoy reading the dirt about their idol as well as all the trivia. Perhaps someone in the class can explain this apparent contradiction.

Reading fan magazines is one way to discover something about the psychology of an idolater. For a small sum of money, perhaps five or six shillings, the fan will get a membership card, an

[1] Goodman.

information sheet, pictures, and regular bulletins. These are chatty: the star acknowledges gifts he has been sent, describes the latest stage of his professional career, and prints a selection of letters, in answer to some of which he offers avuncular advice. These bulletins do not dwell on some of the more extraordinary activities of the fans: the requests for old tooth-brushes, chewing-gum or cigarette butts, the offers of marriage or fanatical love. They may occasionally mildly rebuke fans, should the need arise, for having torn the star's suits to shreds or bruised him in their frantic efforts to touch the divine presence. This adulation can go on after death: James Dean received more fan mail after his death than any film star who was alive at the time. There were many requests for a piece of his car, and many letters were quite certain that the hero was not dead, but merely in hiding, ashamed of his terrible scars. For those who reluctantly accepted that he was no more, 'One Los Angeles firm was doing roaring trade with three-inch-high cast stone heads of Dean. Another concern was marketing a life-size head of the actor, finished in miracle-flesh, a plastiflex material that looked and felt like human flesh, so that his fans could even fondle Dean if they so desired!'[1]

This situation is worrying to anyone concerned with education, though it is fair to point out that some fan clubs are active in adopting charities. It is true that many pupils do not fall for all this ballyhoo; but the few who do are very often the quiet ones with a strong desire to escape into a fantasy world. Some fantasy during adolescence is unavoidable, and no one would wish to be censorious over it. But it is harmful when a fan starts living through the body and motions of her favourite star, who may not be a very real person anyhow. The teacher cannot wade in and strip pupils of their illusions brutally and quickly. His approach should be gradual and understanding. Most of his pupils will be healthily sceptical about the whole system anyhow, but there will be others who will need more careful handling. The teacher should invite them to think about these

[1] Goodman.

points, and ask them to treat their reading matter more analytically, and to show him any results they may have reached. What were the last ten stories you read about the star? Do you believe them? Why do fans get so keen on someone? Is it a real person they are in love with, or a myth? How much of it is done to keep in with the other people in the class? This last question is a real one, as I have several times come across clear cases of a sort of conformity, where the pupil actually disliked the star, but has carried on worshipping for fear of feeling different. In a school where the children have many home interests, one finds adolescent girls keen on Shakespearian actors, opera singers, ballet dancers, and horses as well as the various pop stars! This variety is good, and can have a stimulating effect on the others. But pupils from working-class homes often have the same uniform interests; if it is not one pop singer, it will be another. They have been well and truly brain-washed. And it is for the teacher to show the doubters that there may be far better things to give their interest to than the star whom they meekly follow with the others. There are a few films available that show the reactions of teenage girls to pop singers, and there is no reason why these should not be shown to the class.

In another context, Morin quotes some pathetic letters in which teenage worshippers confess that they will never be interested in any other man, and that, even when they are kissing their boy friends, they are really imagining it to be their favourite star. Pupils may feel embarrassed by some of this; but no teacher likes to think of his pupils living vicariously through someone else, and the real fans should have the experience of seeing themselves as others see them. When the teacher feels it is the right time, he can show the class *We are the Lambeth Boys*, which gives a rollicking if slightly bowdlerised version of London teenagers, and certainly bears the message that the real is always preferable to the myth. After it I ask the pupils to write an essay about themselves and the area they live in called 'We are the...Boys'. It usually works, and I get essays about people and experiences that are real and living. Pupils always have a lot to say about stars and the star system, and there is much to be talked and written about. Film magazines, fan magazines, show-business columns, and impressions of the stars themselves all make excellent material for lessons, and pupils should be encouraged to bring them to school, and to use them in the many ways a teacher can suggest.

I have mentioned film criticism and its obvious uses in building up film appreciation. There are three sorts of film criticism: general reviews, trade reviews, and advertisements (including trailers, posters, or displays in the press).

General press reviews range from the good to the very bad. Pupils should collect them, and by comparing them with films they have seen should learn which critics they think they can trust. Individual critics' strengths and weaknesses can be extremely revealing. Trade reviews are addressed not to the general public, but to hard-headed distributors who want good box-office returns. Thus *A Diary of a Nudist* is succinctly described as 'Dialogue trite but nudes ungainly', and the box-office angle is described as 'Title sucker bait solely for small industrial halls' (elsewhere referred to as 'The cap and muffler trade'). *Girl on The Road* has 'compelling feminine slant and big promotion angles'; *Death Comes From Outer Space* is summed up as 'Nuclear Thriller, "U" certificate. Good mass entertainment. Excellent for Children'. Sometimes the descriptions have their own humour. *Der Rosenkavalier* is described as a 'gay ear-tickling operetta, and outstanding British prestige musical . . . by the way, there are three acts, and the two intervals should certainly create a demand for chocolates and ice-cream'.

Trailers, posters, and advertisements, on the other hand, paint a quite different picture, and can hardly be trusted at all. Everything is superlative, and is given a violent, erotic, or horrific twist. Erotic posters refer to female stars as 'Magnificent human animals', or 'Marie-the-body-Macdonald', and the poster illustrations show a lot of what the Americans call 'chest art'. They belong to the old tradition of showmanship, where almost anything goes. We can read suggestions for extra publicity in the trade press. 'A street stunt was operated by an attractive model in Western costume, who fired a blank loaded gun every twenty seconds to attract the attention of passers-by.' In Amsterdam a comedian advertised *Sodom and Gomorrah* by auctioning six models dressed in slaves' robes. For sheer verbal horror consider the suggestion for a slogan promoting the film *Ulysses*—'U'll see Ulysses'. All these sources can be used together to make an interesting and often revealing picture of a film, which looks well on a classroom wall. A press review, a trade review, an advertisement, and finally a pupil's own assessment put together into one block can make useful reading.

RUNNING A SCHOOL FILM SOCIETY

A film society can be one of the school's most important extra-curricular activities; even without a systematic screen education, much can be achieved in this way. It is an excellent chance to show films that many pupils would never see for themselves, and their effect can be quite startling. Eight films in each season are generally enough: four before and four after Christmas. Choice of films will depend on how much money is available; new Technicolor films, for example, cost a great deal. Some of the bigger distributors, noticeably Rank, Warner-Pathé, Ron Harris, and Contemporary, offer a block-booking scheme, which can reduce costs. Should money run out before the end of the season, there are some excellent free films that can be obtained from Fords, British Transport, Shell, Philip's Electric, the Gas Council, and the Petroleum Film Bureau, as well as the Polish, Indian, Dutch, and Swedish embassies.

The teacher may feel like choosing all the films himself, but this has its dangers, and is not good practice. Far better to have a pupils' committee which is aware of the expenses and chooses accordingly. If a block-booking scheme is being worked, choice will be limited to one catalogue. Otherwise, there might be an arrangement by which the teacher and the committee share the choice of film, or agree to show eight different types of film to ensure variety. Posters for publicity can be hired from B.F.I., but it is obviously better to get school artists to design them. Committee members may have their own high-powered ideas for recruitment, should numbers fall short.

After the film has been shown, there should certainly be a discussion, but on another day, possibly in the lunch hour, when pupils do not have to hurry off home, and have had time to digest what they have seen. This discussion can be led by the teacher, or, better still, by a committee member. Other teachers who have been persuaded to stay behind to see the film can also be asked to make guest contributions. With enough enthusiasm, the society can organise one or two school outings. It is difficult to get permission to go round a film studio, but there are other pleasant visits possible: a trip to the occasional cinema which offers special film shows in the morning, or an evening out at the town cinema.

MAKING A FILM

This is a very important part of a screen education course, and allows pupils to put into practice some of the ideas and knowledge gained during the year. As an activity, it fits very well into the summer term. The film may be made during school time with the teacher's own class, or after school with a broader cast, possibly of film society members. The difficulty is not the expense; camera equipment can sometimes be hired fairly cheaply, and the whole cost of making a four minute film need not exceed £10. The difficulty lies much more in organisation and getting a good shooting script. The best and most complete guide to the whole process can be found in *Young Film Makers* by Don Waters and Sydney Rees, both experts at school film making.

The first stage is obviously to choose a good story. Pupils will probably begin by suggesting over-ambitious themes, and it is as well to remind them that the film will be silent, and, because of expense, will not last very long. (I have found that a four-minute film can be quite long enough for pupils who are just beginning.) Thus the plot will have to be a clear and fairly simple one which will be conveyed by the pictures in the frame alone, since no one wants to interrupt a film with patches of written dialogue or explanations. The best story will emerge from the pupils' own experience, which will be genuine and can be shot in the area around the school. For silent films, comedies are better than tragedies, which tend to become very melo-dramatic, and a brisk functional approach is better than dreamy 'poetic' images, which can look very pretentious at this stage. Above all, the film should not be 'educational' in the narrow sense of the word. The teacher should certainly keep an eye over all proceedings, and should help pupils to organise themselves, but the story should be left to the class, since no one wants any more school-inspired films about Sports Day or the School Camp.

Before the film is even thought of, pupils should see some other films made by children, which are available from the B.F.I. They will soon realise the difference between laughing *at* a film and laughing *with* it, and the absolute necessity of having a good story and script. This, by far the most difficult task, is best done in the classroom, with everyone giving their own ideas. Most of these will be impractical, and soon pupils will begin to realise the real nature of their task. When about three good ideas have finally emerged, the teacher might ask for these to be prepared in more detail, and eventually the class, or group, can vote on the one it likes best.

The next stage is to prepare a shooting script and to see that pupils are appointed to different jobs. At this stage, a director and his assistant will be needed. The director must be a good organiser, and able to control a situation that often seems to threaten anarchy. It is essential that everyone should know what his job is, and what it entails. Besides seeing to this, the director's other task will be to assist the script-writer in breaking down the story into different shots, specifying the camera distance for each separate shot, saying what the shot is going to show, and how long it will last. Thus there will be no danger of film running out before the story is ended; indeed, the wise director will always have up to twice as much film as the story requires, to cover retakes as well as general mistakes and emergencies.

Casting is a most difficult job, since no one can afford film for screen tests. But as Waters and Rees point out, it is often the more retiring pupil who makes the best and most restrained screen actor. Another problem is the actors' wardrobe: it is essential that each character has the same clothes each time he is filmed, and it is sometimes practical to keep his film clothes at school, on hand for filming.

Continuity is one of the biggest difficulties, and gives enough work for at least three people. One of these can make a point of recording the action involved in each shot, while another must do the routine work involving position and clothes. 'Light' continuity when working outside is also important, and a light meter is quite essential to get consistency. It is not necessary, as many people believe, to wait for the sun to shine before filming need start, but it is essential to adjust the lens should filming have begun in darker weather.

The camera also needs its own crew. One boy must look after the tripod, and adjust it for each different shot. Another must estimate the distance for each shot, using a 'tape' if necessary. A third will be in charge of the stop-watch to time each shot, and a fourth must chalk up the number of each shot, which must be recorded on film before each scene begins, in order to help the editing at the end of the film.

If filming is going to be indoors, some lightsmen will be needed. Waters and Rees recommend photoflood lamps with a silvered surface, and go on to make useful technical recommendations for improving on them. Perhaps for a first attempt, however, the film should be kept out of doors, where there is plenty of room for everyone to make as much noise as they like.

When shooting the film, there is no need to take each scene in the order in which it appears in the script. Similar scenes should be taken together, which will save time. Lots of rehearsal is needed, both for the actors and for the technical crew. When a scene is ready, there should be a final 'dry run' before the camera actually takes it. Pupils should always start acting before the camera begins; although it will be a silent film, they should of course talk quite naturally. If a scene just filmed is clearly no good, or if the director suspects that it could have been better, he should retake it, providing of course that he has enough film.

There are many other points that may have to be learnt by experience. Someone will forget to wind the camera before shooting; or, even worse, the cover will be left on the lens. Despite the best organisation, someone will forget to adjust the lens after a close-up, or will misread the light meter. It is important to point out to pupils that faults of workmanship can ruin an otherwise good film and can alienate the most tolerant of audiences. All instructions and checks should be carried out very thoroughly—and then gone through once more.

When the camera has been unloaded and the film sent off and processed, it is time for editing. Again, this is very hard work. All the shots must be cut up and spliced in their correct order. The editor must decide which is the best shot to use, and where the best place is to make a cut. That is why it is essential to work with 16 millimetre film, since with anything smaller editing is practically impossible. For really successful editing the class will need an animated viewer, and Waters and Rees discuss fully this and other ways of editing a film.

Finally the film will be ready for public showing, and if it is a success it can be entered for the annual Young Film Makers Competition, sponsored by the National Union of Teachers. The whole operation can be extremely exciting, and it is also a very good lesson for the pupils in learning how to work with film and with each other. They can use some of the knowledge and insight they have gained during the year through films shown and discussed at school. In the end they may make a film that is really worthwhile and an exciting ending for what is often their last term at school.

Lastly, Tony Hodgkinson in *Screen Education*, 14, has described another type of film which schools can make, where children are asked to draw, paint or scribble with photographic colouring inks on a length of clear transparent celluloid. This technique has been perfected by a Canadian film maker, Norman McClaren, and some of his films are available from the B.F.I. When the film is projected, pupils will see a fast-moving abstract colour film, which may look even better if it is shown with a jazz record as an accompaniment. Later they can experiment, and with enough patience can present some sort of crude animation, although this will give only one second's film for every 32 animated frames. This sort of animation will have to be elementary, like two dots moving round the frame, but it can be amusing and delights younger children.

CHAPTER IV

TELEVISION

Before we decide to teach television appreciation and discrimination in the classroom, it would be as well to know the size of the audience we shall be catering for. Will such lessons be unfair on those children whose parents do not own a set? This is hardly a problem for teachers in most parts of Britain. In 1963 86 per cent of the population owned sets, and Dr Himmelweit, in the classic Nuffield study *Television and the Child*, puts the child's average viewing at about two hours a day.

In a spot check carried out by the B.B.C.'s audience research survey one Friday at 8.30 p.m., it was ascertained that 61 per cent of all children aged between 5 and 14 were watching television at that time. (The figure for children between 12 and 14 was 71 per cent.) In fact, before 9 o'clock both B.B.C. and I.T.A. maintain an informal 'Family viewing' policy, under which they do not show programmes which might be considered unsuitable for children. After this time, first consideration is given to the adult viewer home from work, even though it is known that youngsters are still watching (in fact three out of four children of 10 and 11 watch up to 9 o'clock, and some much later). It is, of course, a difficult problem; the television companies have solved it for themselves by saying that although some programmes may be unsuitable for children who may still be viewing, it is for the parents to guide the children's choice. This is hardly an effective argument: many children view programmes when their parents are not there, and in many homes the television set is the focal point of the room, so that if one person is watching a programme, everybody else does too.[1]

[1] Yet there is a drop in children watching on their own after the end of children's programmes, and it is hard to see how TV can ever really solve this problem of when to show programmes suitable only for adults, when the audience at home can be so unselective.

What sort of programmes can most children see, and what is their effect likely to be? It has become slightly old-fashioned to talk of the 'effect' of television on children, since so many ridiculous prophecies were once made, including more divorce, illiteracy, attempted suicides, nightmares and tooth decay. The effect of television is far more intangible, and so far no one has been able to prove anything really positive one way or the other. This is no excuse for the complacency many producers seem to feel about their programmes; as Dr Himmelweit has pointed out, it is not enough for television to prove merely that it does no harm, but also that it can do some good.[1] What, if any, is their programmes' stimulation effect on the thoughts and imagination? It may well be that harm is done not by what young people watch, but by the amount of time they watch television (although to be fair, children who are now compulsive viewers seem in pre-television days to have been compulsive comic-readers instead).

So long as its effect for good or bad is still a matter for speculation, the teacher is free to come to his own conclusions and act accordingly. The situation facing him is that, in general, older children's favourites are the 'top twenty' most popular programmes, as assessed by TAM (television audience measurement) each week. Those occasionally vary but generally include 'soap operas', Westerns, crime serials, games and quizzes. Such programmes, though well produced, are not usually considered by critics to be of very high quality, and are often described as trivial, facile, and sometimes violent. They are usually shown at peak viewing times, between 7 and 9 o'clock. When this is pointed out, the providers may sometimes admit that such programmes may have little intrinsic value, but say the public must be given what it wants. This is disingenuous: the public is made up of minorities as well as majorities, and there is no reason why minority programmes should always be at inconvenient times. TAM ratings alone can be a very

[1] 'Television Research and Action.' A chapter in *The Social Impact of Film and Television on Youth* (UNESCO).

blunt instrument for measuring public opinion: many good popular programmes began with small audiences; and one wonders whether, with the tyranny of TAM ratings, and the continual necessity to show advertisers that enough people are watching the set at one particular time, such experimental programmes will be allowed to happen again. Instead the public is given at peak hours programmes which are known to be safe bets for large audiences—and which therefore tend to be unadventurous and repetitive. Viewers who are critical—and since TAM ratings only reflect the size of an audience, not the strength of its opinions, there may be more of these than one thinks—are always told that they can simply turn off the set or switch over. But, as Mr R. J. E. Silvey, head of B.B.C. audience research, has pointed out, channel loyalty appears to be becoming another part of the complexity of our class system. Habitual B.B.C. and I.T.V. viewers tend to regard the other channel with suspicion and prejudice.[1] Rather than switch over, such viewers will often stick it out with a programme they might not even like, convinced that the B.B.C. is *always* highbrow, or I.T.V. *always* vulgar. They could, of course, switch off, but this seems an exercise in self-control beyond some people. Rather, they will do something else and keep half an eye on the set; Mr Silvey has estimated that about one in four viewers is doing something else while viewing, such as eating a meal, sewing or even reading.

The situation then is that most children spend a great deal of valuable leisure time watching television, without any obvious gain. Dr Himmelweit found that little information was retained by children from programmes, mainly because of the quick change from one programme to another. Miss Muriel Telford, headmistress of Leek High School for girls, has examined this situation eloquently. 'Unless and until we train ourselves to switch off smartly, no opportunity occurs for assimilation of the programme just finished, for criticism or discussion of it,

---

[1] This was written before the opening of a third channel—B.B.C. 2—on April 20, 1964.

or even simply for pleasurable recollection. More important, we have not the time or opportunity (without which we shall frequently make fools of ourselves) for adjustment to a different type of programme and a different level of realism.'[1] The same phenomenon, where television is treated as a continual chatter-box, rather than a medium capable of being taken seriously, has been found with some adult viewing. Dr Himmelweit reports on a 'before and after' study of selected viewers who saw a programme on capital punishment.[2] The results were disappointing; some of the most elementary facts had completely escaped the viewers' notice, and they could be considered only a fraction better informed than they had been before.

If the teacher is concerned that television is being used by his pupils merely 'to distract, amuse, and insulate', his duty is clear: he must help his pupils not only to discriminate against some programmes but also to appreciate others. There are, of course, some excellent programmes on all channels; it would be sad if they were swamped by the general flood of 'vague and puerile programmes, whose contents are often derivative, repetitious and lacking in real substance'.[3]

'There is also in our view a duty on those who are charged with the responsibility for education to see that teenagers who are at the most insecure and suggestible stage of their lives, are not suddenly exposed to the full force of the mass media without some counter-balancing assistance.' Few would quarrel with this quotation from the Crowther Report, but teachers have been slow to respond to the challenge of television. Dr Himmel-weit found, in a survey of teachers, that only 6 per cent bothered to talk to their classes about television. It may be that there is a wide gap between the teacher's preferences, should he have a television set, and those of his class. Tony Hodgkinson suggests a way of bridging this gap. 'I am inclined to suggest that, for the first six months at least, you should let the children guide your viewing, and watch what they recommend. It will help

---

[1] *Screen Education*, 11.   [2] *The Social Impact of Film and Television on Youth*.
[3] *Report of the Committee on Broadcasting* (Pilkington Report).

them in acting as your guides, and by trying humbly to discover "what they see in it" you will learn a great deal. You will also better appreciate the difficulty of your open-minded pupils who dutifully sit in front of the programme you recommend and try to discover "what Sir sees in this".[1]

But whatever methods he uses, the teacher must try, and he would be unwise to leave his efforts too long. 'By the age of fifteen,' the UNESCO report states, 'young people show what might be called adult taste in their choice of television programmes. Their taste seems to become more or less stabilized .... It means above all that efforts must be made to cultivate a child's taste when he is eight years old and not when he is an adolescent of fifteen years. By then it is too late.'

It is clear, then, that if the teacher is going to have any effect he must start early and teach consistently. Unlike some television companies, he can be uninhibited in what he says: he does not have to worry about making a profit. He is faced by a medium of uncertain power; in most cases his pupils will be watching it for far longer hours than they watch him. His chief task is to establish that television is something to be discussed, rather than passively accepted. These discussions may lead to a host of youngsters round his desk after the lesson is over, talking about things they have recently seen, since for many pupils a formal lesson period still lays a dead hand on free discussion. The teacher may long to go for his lunch or cup of tea, but he will also know that the most important part of his lesson has just begun.

THE B.B.C. AND I.T.A.

It is important for pupils to understand and to take notes on the constitutions of the B.B.C. and I.T.A. At the moment there is enormous ignorance on the whole topic, and I have often heard pupils complain about all those advertisements on I.T.V., and wish they could either be dropped or pushed on to the B.B.C.!

[1] *The Film Teacher's Handbook, 1959.*

114

The B.B.C. is incorporated by Royal Charter and is a single organisation in the charge of a board of nine governors (appointed by Orders in Council) who are not broadcasters. The B.B.C. director-general's policy must be approved by the governors, and he must have constant access to the chairman. The B.B.C. is independent of the government except for ultimate ministerial powers; this means that the corporation is independent in the conduct of its everyday business, but that since it is dependent on the licence to broadcast granted by the Postmaster-General, parliament still has ultimate power. In fact the Postmaster-General only uses this power to prohibit the B.B.C. from giving its own opinions on current affairs or public policy, and to prohibit party political broadcasts other than those reached in agreement with the leading political parties. The B.B.C., like I.T.A., has frequent programmes where broadcasters can give their own views on current affairs, and there are also plenty of programmes with a political approach which do not qualify as party political broadcasts. In return, the Postmaster-General is responsible for collecting licence revenue, and occasionally he has to answer criticisms in parliament of the B.B.C.'s service. Here, either he insists that this is a matter for the B.B.C. alone, or while still maintaining this, he will nevertheless give an answer based on information gathered from the B.B.C. 'The independence of the B.B.C. from government and parliament is accepted everywhere as fundamental to British broadcasting.'[1]

The preamble to the B.B.C.'s charter refers to the value of the services 'as a means of disseminating information, education, and entertainment', and exactly the same phrase can now be found in the 1964 Television Act defining the function of the I.T.A. By dicussing the constitution of the B.B.C., pupils will now know why their parents pay licence money, and there is no harm in a class debating whether it gets its money's worth, provided the teacher is there to correct misunderstandings and discourage red herrings. To begin with, many pupils

[1] *Report of the Committee on Broadcasting* (Pilkington Report).

are strongly prejudiced against the B.B.C. Whether this prejudice becomes modified or not depends very much on the teacher and his lessons.

The I.T.A. is a state corporation answerable to, yet independent of, the government, much like the B.B.C. There are 13 members of the authority, and it functions as a regulatory body in so far as it grants contracts to programme contractors whom it thinks will produce programmes of a satisfactory standard. (Though the authority has a conditional power to produce its own programmes, it has never yet done this.) The authority has power to require that nothing shall be broadcast without its previous approval, and discusses each company's quarterly programme schedule in advance. It requires that certain programmes be transmitted by all companies, and that programme schedules be balanced, and contain a due amount of serious programmes. The I.T.A. has the power to levy fines for breaches of taste, and also to refuse renewal of contracts—which would be such a serious step that it is doubtful whether it would ever be taken.

The big companies which own these contracts are familiar to all viewers. A.B.C. Television provides programmes in the Midlands and North during week-ends, Rediffusion Television Limited covers London's weekdays, Associated Television Limited covers London's week-ends and the Midlands' weekdays, while Granada T.V. Network covers the North's weekdays. These are the 'big four'. As well as these, we also have the 'little ten' which cover regional areas not included by the big four. Here we have Southern Television (central, southern, and south-east England), Westward Television (south-west England), Anglia Television (East Anglia), Tyne-Tees Television (north-east England), T.W.W. (South Wales and the West of England), Ulster Television (Northern Ireland), Border Television (the borders), Scottish Television (central Scotland), Grampian Television (north-east Scotland), Channel Television (the Channel Islands). This arrangement is easier to understand when the areas are shaded on a map, and the exact areas can be found in the I.T.V. year book. All these companies guarantee transmission in the hours allotted to broadcasting, and they themselves let advertising time to advertising agencies or to individual advertisers. Many pupils will immediately point out that they have seen, for instance, Granada programmes on a London set. This is because of the highly complex system of *networking*, by which all the I.T.A.'s transmitting stations are joined to one another by cable or radio link. Thus a programme produced by one company can be seen in areas served by other companies. The I.T.A. has stated that a certain amount of broadcasting time should originate from each company, major or regional, and that a suitable proportion of this should appeal especially to regional tastes and outlook. Five per cent of total transmission time is taken up by the news broadcasts produced by Independent Television News and networked all over the country. The rest of the available time is shared by agreement between the big four: on weekdays Granada and Rediffusion Television get four-fifths of it, and Associated Television one-fifth. At week-ends, A.T.V. and A.B.C. make a similar arrangement. Apart from the news, the little ten are not bound to take the network programmes, but they almost invariably do take some, since otherwise they must produce their own programme or use an old one; it is thus generally uneconomic for regional companies to produce more than their minimum contractual obligation of broadcasting time.

Pupils all over the British Isles can use this knowledge to great effect. Is there a 'product pattern' in the programme produced by any of the big four or the little ten? In what way do they serve their region's special interest, and are they successful in doing this? (Details of these programmes can be found in the I.T.V. handbook and in the daily press.) Which in their opinion is the best of the companies, and which is the worst? Why?

As we have seen, the Television Act of 1964 defines the purpose of the medium as 'information, education and entertainment', and it was also laid down 'that the programmes maintain a proper balance in their subject matter, and a high general standard of quality'. Although any assessment of quality is bound to be subjective, any pupil can quickly discover whether a proper balance is being presented. They will need a copy of the *Radio Times* and the appropriate I.T.V. guide, which they should in any case be encouraged to have at home, to aid them in their selection of programmes. The work can be done in the book in which they keep their television diary. First of all, it will be necessary to divide programmes into various types. Although categories are bound to be somewhat arbitrary, it is convenient to divide programmes into two sorts; serious and light. (Plays can be either serious or light, so it is best not to attempt a grouping in this case. Educational broadcasts take up the same amount of time on both services, so they can be omitted too.) Here is a list of 'serious' and 'light' programmes, based on work done in the Pilkington Report.

Serious Programmes

1. News and current affairs.
2. Talks and discussions.
3. Documentaries.
4. Outside broadcasting of important non-sporting events.
5. Serious music.
6. Opera and ballet.
7. Religion.

Light Programmes

1. Light comedy.
2. Sport.
3. Variety programmes (including quizzes and panel games).
4. Light music and songs.
5. Travel programmes.
6. 'Real Life' serials.
7. Western and crime films.

Using the *Radio Times* and *TV Times*, the teacher can then ask the class to compare the number of hours spent each week by the two services on these types of programmes, category by category. Again, this is a most useful exercise, since pupils will have to use their own criteria for categorising various programmes, and will therefore be making judgements of some use to them. When this is done, the class should also compare programmes showing at 'peak' hours, the time when about 80 per cent of homes with television are watching one or other of the services. This is nearly always between 8 and 10 p.m. when up to nine million families may be watching. When they have done this, the class will be better able to assess which service offers a better balanced diet, both in the long run and during peak hours.

There are other shorter exercises interesting for a class of television viewers. Television is often spoken of as a 'live' medium. In fact, only about 40 per cent of B.B.C. programmes are broadcast live, and even these often have some scenes on film and video tape. Indeed, many of our common assumptions about television as a whole need inspection. Is it really a visual medium first of all, or does it depend far more than people imagine on what the audience *hears*? This can be tested by asking pupils to try to do without the vision or sound for one programme, and seeing which of them get the best idea of what is supposed to be happening. It is an instructive exercise in many ways!

The I.T.A. has contracted not to use more than 14 per cent of foreign material, about three-quarters of which would be of American origin, but during peak hours the percentage of American material rises above this figure. Is this the same on B.B.C.? Does the class find this a particularly pleasing state of affairs? Can any pupil discover, perhaps by getting in touch with the organisations, which British programmes sell best abroad?

There is often argument about the idea of a 'natural break' in the middle of programmes for advertisements. Breaks are

9

deemed by I.T.A. to be unnatural when they come in the middle of news bulletins, football matches (during play), and discussions. They are not unnatural between stages of a quiz, the acts of a play, the rounds of a boxing match, half-time at a football match, and in a film when there is a 'significant change in scene or lapse of time'. Pupils can be made aware of these nuances, and can be their own judges of whether these terms are being respected. They should particularly look out for plays and films that have been constructed to include natural breaks.

TELEVISION TECHNIQUE

Understanding the technique of a programme is quite ancillary to understanding its broader aspects, but when children have become used to watching television with half their attention, an interest in technique will help them to watch more closely. Stereotyped technique can lead to equally dull programmes; the class will understand this better when it can see the relationship between the two. Equally, a sensitive technique can contribute a lot to our enjoyment. Albert Casey, writing in *Screen Education*, 16, brings out this point well. Describing *Z Cars*, an outstanding B.B.C. serial about Liverpool policemen, and comparing it with *No Hiding Place*, a routine serial thriller, he says:

The screen is alive in a way that is rare on T.V. This is due to a number of things. The six cameras are fully used, giving a variety of set-ups and many more separate shots than one would normally expect. There are well-constructed sets which give a depth to the picture, and the film sequences are expertly cut in, maintaining the fluid movement. A great deal of the deadness of T.V. comes from a lack of attention to these qualities. During the last transmission of *Z Cars* I switched over to *No Hiding Place*. Within minutes I had seen several conversations shot from a frontal position against a background of wall, window and curtains, and the abruptness of the film sequence was underlined by the accompanying canned music. Just before the commercial break there was the inevitable key line equally inevitably emphasised by the track-in of the camera and the dramatic music.

In order to grasp detailed points of this nature, pupils are helped by having an understanding of the techniques involved, and a vocabulary with which to discuss them. In any case, pupils of all ages like to hear 'how it is done'; and provided he keeps such discussion within its proper limits, the teacher can always put such lessons to some constructive use.

The whole business of producing a play makes a good introduction to the different departments of a television studio. The producer, who supplies the funds, will appoint a particular director to look after a programme. The director's responsibilities are enormous: he has to supervise the operational side of the programme, and is answerable for its final appearance. In every way he is a key figure, and pupils will do well to know some of the directors' names and the sort of work they produce. The director must first get in touch with the writer to go over the script with him. If the script-writer is experienced there may not be many alterations to make, since writing for television is a highly skilled and specialised job. Aristotle's unities of time, place and action have a particular significance in this medium; time-lags are difficult to convey, so time is usually continuous, while too many sets will confuse an audience and are in any case impossible in a small studio. Many plays do not use more than four sets, and will make do with pre-filmed shots for any further extension of place; but film is expensive and can disturb the rhythm of the action, so writers try to avoid too many outdoor scenes. Again, too many characters in a complex story are confusing on a small screen, so the writer generally concentrates on one main story, with perhaps two main characters. All this obviously influences the nature of his stories and their plots. There is no room for a *Ben Hur* on television: the actors have not enough room, and the whole medium is too small and constricting for huge crises and emotions. Television lends itself far better to intimate treatment of themes that remind us of everyday crises, rather than something magnificent or exotic; its normal means of communication is by the close-up, and the closer together two characters are on the set, the less stress is laid upon dialogue, as the writer can rely upon their faces to tell the story. This dependence on the close-up limits the range of things a writer can do, but also can give his work a subtlety which might be difficult to achieve on a large cinema screen.

Within these limitations the writer has to establish a time, some characters, their relationships and a plot which are all sufficiently clear and interesting to hold an audience which may consist of millions but is made up of small family groups, each sitting round their set. In order to capture their attention, some writers feel they have to begin their play with a minor sensation or some extremely odd situation. This method has its limitations; the teacher can point out that there are other more subtle ways of establishing interest in a play. What sort of people are the characters and how do we know? What is their relationship to each other and what is supposed to have happened before the action of the play begins? By thinking about this sort of question many pupils will become interested in the gradual unfolding of a plot, where they might before have either switched off or tried another channel. If pupils do see a play which they enjoy, they should certainly remember the name of the script-writer for further reference. There are also several published editions of television plays, in which all these principles can be seen in more detail.

When the director casts the play, he must choose actors who are really familiar with the medium, and who know how essential it is to keep an exact position on the set, since every move will have been worked out in detail beforehand. An actor must not 'mask' his colleagues, walk out of camera range, or move away from his scenery. He must remember which of the many cameras is filming him, and whether he is in close-up, since a camera many yards away with a telescopic 'zoom' lens can get this effect as well as a camera almost next to him. It is easy for an actor to forget the zoom range, and to walk right out of a shot, leaving the cameraman struggling behind him. He must also learn to delay his reactions just a fraction more than he would in the theatre, since he must wait for the camera to switch over to him before he begins any given reaction. Scenes sometimes begin 'cold' in the middle of a crisis or action, which is a strain on an actor who likes to work up to an atmosphere. Most of his acting will be done in close-up, where melodramatic tricks will be quickly obvious. Pupils will gladly discuss their favourite television actors, all of whom will overcome these difficulties in their own individual way.

While the play is still in rehearsal, the designer will be finishing his sets. It is very important for the audience to know where the action is supposed to be happening, and what information this sheds on the characters. In this way, each different set will be telling part of the story. The designer must achieve the maximum effect in as little space as possible, because sets are expensive and studio space is very limited and cannot take a very large set. Some designers tackle this by cramming as much detail as possible into a small space, but more skilful designers achieve the same realism more sparingly, and their sets never have a 'larger than life' feeling. An immediate problem to a designer is the floor: carpets and tiles are impractical in a studio, and he may have to use a large floor painting to get the same effect.

If the director wants to use film made previously on location, the designer must make sure that it will not clash with his studio sets, and that characters will be able, for example, to walk through French windows on to a wide lawn without anybody noticing that film has taken over from studio. He can also create exteriors by 'back projection', where a film of scenery or a moving scene is projected from behind on to a screen. This can be placed at a window or door of the set, and it will seem as if we are looking out to sea, at passing clouds, or at whatever is desired; it is used particularly in scenes set in cars, planes and trains, where scenery flashes by outside the window. If the designer wants to establish scenery which can remain static, he will use enormous photographs, which when skilfully lit will appear like the real thing. There is also a technique for front projection: if an effect like fire, rain or fog is desired, it can be suggested by superimposing a continuous film 'loop' of the phenomenon on to the normal camera shots.

If it is kept going too long, however, the audience may begin to spot the pattern, as the same flames will be seen coming up over and over again.

Throughout his preparations, the designer must work very closely with the lighting engineer, who has another difficult job. Spotlights cannot be used to any great extent in television studios, so it is extremely difficult to emphasise any particular detail. Light can seldom give the dramatic effects we can expect in the cinema as it is much more diffuse. The lighting engineer must make sure that the scenery is lit in a convincing way; if the designer has pushed the sets almost to the studio walls, he will not have enough room for good back lighting, and the scenery might look dark and unconvincing. When the director decides to use film made separately on location, then the lighting on the set must be exactly like that in the film. Some temperamental film stars have their own favourite lighting engineer, who knows exactly which of their features looks best, and how to light it. Television stars cannot be quite as fussy; the lighting engineer must do the best he can. If he does his job well, we should hardly be aware of him; if not, his efforts may appear obtrusive and possibly melodramatic—often the case when the material itself is poor anyhow, and the lighting effects are trying to compensate for the lack of real drama in the script.

After perhaps three weeks' rehearsals the play may be ready for transmission. The director will be in a control room, over-looking the studio floor. He is in contact through earphones with the floor manager, who is responsible for seeing that the props are in the correct positions, for cueing the various performers and by vigorous hand signals showing them where they have to go, and how much time they have. The director also communicates with the cameramen, also through ear-phones; not a word is heard on the studio floor by anybody else. Apart from the actors, everyone else must move in absolute silence during performance; the cameras track in and out noiselessly, while technicians pad by on rubber-soled shoes.

Only a viewer with extremely perceptive hearing would be aware of the occasional minor collision or squeak which can happen even in the best ordered studio.

In his control room, the director usually has four line monitors in front of him, each of which transmits a picture from one of the four cameras. From these four pictures, the director chooses one to transmit to the home audience, while the other three cameras maintain their pictures in readiness for the time when the director may wish to cut from one camera to another. This process of cutting is by far the most difficult skill the director has to learn. Basically, he should cut to a different picture just when most of us would wish him to. If he cuts too quickly and aimlessly, he can disturb and irritate the viewer: this is called 'switcher's twitch'; if he cuts too little he may bore us with a prolonged picture from only one angle. There are a host of other points he must remember, which he has to work out in rehearsal. If there is music, he may have to cut in time to it. The audience must be given an 'establishing shot' every now and again, to remind them of the sort of room, and the sort of atmosphere the characters are meeting in, and where they stand in relation to each other. This establishing shot is usually a general view of the scene, and we often have one on the exit or entrance of a character. If the director wishes to cut from a camera at the right, he must be very careful that the audience does not become disoriented, and sees characters who were looking to the left of their screen suddenly looking to the right. The same problem crops up with movement. If actors are walking from the left of the picture to the right, it would not do to cut to another view which showed them walking in the opposite direction. But if he is cutting from one camera to another on the same side, he must be careful that this does not make the characters seem to give little jumps to a slightly different position on the picture.

Another problem in a live broadcast is simply getting an actor from one set to another, should he have to appear again immediately in the next scene. Sometimes the script-writer will help; after ushering out the main character, perhaps with an 'I'll see you out', a supporting actor will take a moment to arrange flowers, pat her hair in the mirror or some other minor action, while the star rushes across to the next set. More subtly, the next scene can begin with a close-up, perhaps of someone's hand pouring out a cup of tea, and then we see the star still holding the teapot. But it was not her hands we saw; someone else was doing this while she was running over. This is called a 'cutaway' shot, which is something that appears to be taking place on the set, but will probably be done in a different part of the studio, with the minimum of background filled in to make it appear to belong to the original set. When a star has to change clothes between sets, the problem becomes really difficult and may lead to the show being recorded and not broadcast live. Then, by discontinuous recording, there will be a little more time.

A final problem the director must deal with is sound. Most of us have seen the long 'boom' microphone, which travels above the actors' heads, dip momentarily into the picture. It cannot be used in 'long shots', and sometimes it is unable to reach the back of the studio. When it is impractical to use it, the sound engineer must hide a static microphone behind a picture or in a vase of flowers. Sound is always a problem, and if the viewer turns down the picture for a moment, he will realise how inconsistent the noise level is.

Everything that is sensibly worked out in rehearsal does not necessarily happen on the night itself. A camera may go out of action, or an actor may get a movement or position wrong and put all the camera positions out of place. The director in his box must take these emergencies as they come; there is not a moment when he can let up during the performance. In many ways he is the key figure, since he has a large say in the script, and watches the programme through all its stages until its final transmission. The class would do well to watch out for the different directors and try to spot their individual styles. At best they can produce programmes of very great merit, which may be seen by anything up to twelve million people. Few artists at any stage of history can ever have dreamed of such an audience; the class can discuss whether this opportunity is always well taken. Himmelweit found that points of view expressed in dramatic form had a far greater effect on children's outlook than any other form of presentation. This suggests that directors of plays have an extra responsibility to their audience, since one can discuss in dramatic form ideas and practices that no one would dream of allowing in a serious talk or documentary. I shall discuss this aspect of television later.

The director is no less important in other fields. In a talk between two people and a compère, the director will be in the background, flicking the picture from one camera to another. He must be careful: too much aimless cutting will take our minds off the actual discussion. It is usually done by a director who wants an interesting 'reaction shot' from one of the protagonists while the other is still talking. This is a dubious procedure, and as often as not there is *no* reaction, so the shot and the distraction are wasted. The designer too has to pay a great deal of attention to the studio's appearance in front of the cameras; he knows that the furniture and the style of décor he shows will have some effect on the domestic settings of some viewers. In plays, too, the designs cannot help creating something of a public image.

Single speakers with a prepared speech also have a problem —how to appear natural. Few speakers trust themselves to speak impromptu in front of a camera. Some use a teleprompter —a device under the camera that slowly rolls off the speech in front of them. If the speaker does nothing but follow this, his speech may sound wooden and uninteresting. He may try to sound more natural by interrupting his discourse with hesitations, or by 'Where was I?', but if he does too much of this the teleprompter may get dangerously ahead. Teleprompters are used particularly for programmes that have a large number of pictures, all of which must have special cues from the speaker. In more informal talks, the speaker may use notes, but it is better if he uses these frankly, rather than letting himself peer slyly at them under the desk. In America, President Eisenhower for his pre-election address for the 1956 campaign which, incidentally, was watched by an audience roughly 60 per cent below the average number for entertainment programmes, used large printed cards, known as idiot cards in the trade. On these his main facts and figures had been outlined in gigantic writing to assist his poor eyesight, for if he had worn his customary spectacles he would apparently have harmed his public image.

The newsreader uses a teleprompter and notes, since he is on a very tight time ration, and must give accurate cues for the pictorial material. This is a fascinating programme to watch both for its technical and for its general side. Although television studios get the news as soon as anyone else, there may be delay in getting good film of what has been going on. They may then show some fairly irrelevant piece of film with the news, as an excuse to leave the newscaster's face for a moment. Sometimes the film, which has just been rushed through, will be of very poor quality, although relevant. The director must then decide whether to show it or not. The commentary that goes with the film is very important, in so far as it colours our reactions to the pictures in front of us. In general, both news services have a high reputation for impartiality. Commentaries —and accompanying music—are not always blameless in other respects. The commentary may be a needless observation on obvious points in the picture, while the music may just be preparing us for stereotyped reactions. Bias, as is only natural, will however creep in with the more generalised news programmes. It is always far less evident than in the case of newspapers and magazines, and perhaps for this reason we are less on our guard against it. Is there such a thing as a 'televisual' set of common assumptions, for example in the treatment of eccentrics or off-beat subjects, or does this vary according to the personalities involved? What is the effect on us of seeing a serious—or even a tragic subject, juxtaposed with a flippant one coming straight after it? (rather as in some of the glossy magazine publications, which may have a picture of a starving child on one side of the page, and a full page advertisement for sweets on the other). These questions can never be resolved, but they are surely worth discussing.

The interview is one of the things television can manage better than any other medium. It is also something that can be abused. The interviewer can question many people, but may select only a few for transmission; we must be able to trust him to choose representative people, not just the cranks and eccentrics. We must also trust him to select a reasonable part of the interview for transmission, not something that appears ridiculous by being taken out of context. In a film, *Vox Pop*, on hire from the British Film Institute, showing Alan Whicker interviewing people on their political knowledge, a bizarre effect is achieved by putting the more normal interviews first, and ending with the more incongruous reactions. Alan Whicker also asks some seemingly innocent but loaded questions, and there are one or two 'cut-ins', notably of ducks quacking as an accompaniment to the voice of one of the interviewed people. This sort of thing is crudely amusing, but dangerous. An interviewer knows that the situation often produces a flustered reaction, and it is for him to put the interviewed person at his ease, but not too much, or there is a swing the other way and we may get bumptious over-confidence. In fact the interview is a delicate performance, and the class can be told to watch out for its many finer points. The person interviewed often keeps his eyes on the interviewer—he must be made to look at the camera by phrases like 'Tell the viewer'. The interviewer should go over a few questions before the actual interview, but when it is on the air he should not ask exactly the same questions as he asked in rehearsal, or he will get rather dead-sounding prepared answers. A bad interviewer will go for these prepared answers with 'feed' questions like, 'I expect you have had some amusing experiences' and so on. If his questions are too unexpected, however, he may get no answer at all. He should always listen to the answer he gets, and not ask a prepared question which has no relation to what has been said just before. Nor should he ask the sort of question that can be answered by a flat 'Yes' or 'No', or he will have very monosyllabic interviews. The test of a good interviewer is always the same: does he allow the interviewed person's character to come over on the screen, or does he swamp it with his own?

Interviewers have to be skilled performers. When they know they have only half a minute left, and the director is making frantic 'wind-up' signals, they must finish the interview without any sign of hurry or strain. Less skilled interviewers have their summing-up written before the interview has taken place, and will interrupt the interview half a minute before time is up in order to get it in. (This also happens sometimes when the chairman of a discussion is invited to sum up, and it is always obvious, as it sounds so unnatural.) Finally, after the interview is over, the interviewer may have to repeat some of his questions into the camera. There is a simple reason for this. In an outside interview, there is generally only one camera used, which focuses on the face of the person interviewed. In the editing room, the editor may wish to break this picture with an 'inset' of the interviewer asking one of the questions. So after the interview the interviewer looks into the camera, tries to remember how tall his interviewee was and, with his eyes looking at approximately the right height and with a look of interest on his face, repeats the question which the person interviewed has already answered.

Pupils very much enjoy the idea of an interview, and since nearly all of them will be having at least one with an employer sooner or later, it is not a bad idea to practise with a tape recorder, sometimes in front of the class. It will teach pupils to think and talk more fluently, and will also show them how certain questions and methods of interviewing are easier to reply to than others. The teacher can start by asking the first boy a variant of the 'When did you stop beating your wife?'

type of question. When faced by an interviewer in front of a class, individual pupils will then learn something about the interview situation, and how difficult it sometimes is to think of anything sensible to say to certain types of question.

TOPICS FOR DISCUSSION

The various kinds of programme

Continual discussion is essential in lessons about the mass media. Appreciation is the very last thing that lends itself to an authoritative approach by the teacher. There are no definite answers: the teacher can guide the discussion but cannot impose his opinions. Often the class will know far more about some programmes than he will, and in this case the teacher must also be the learner. 'Remember that you represent authority and that the screen is to the children their own private world, into which you can only get accepted after you have shown your credentials. Don't condemn; don't say, "But surely you were in bed by then"; above all don't say, "The only good programmes are on the B.B.C."'.[1]

There are many different types of lesson about television, but they must all have discussion as their basis. This in itself is something a class may take a long time to get used to, never having imagined previously that television is a thing that can be discussed—especially with a teacher. To begin with, the teacher can persuade the class that programmes can be actively selected, not merely endured. Using the weekly supplement, *TV Today* published in *The Stage*, the *Radio Times*, and I.T.V. journals, he can to some extent advertise good programmes and prepare many of the class to see them. This he can do by wall-displays of coming events, reminders before the end of the lesson, and discussion afterwards. For those who have not seen the programme, other pupils can tell them about it, itself a good exercise. The individual teacher must decide how he manages these discussions, but he should certainly consider using some of the questions investigated by Dr Himmelweit.[2]

[1] *Film Teacher's Handbook, 1959.*
[2] *Television and the Child*

About fiction programmes children were asked: how frequent is aggression by good and bad people, which values find expression and which are not mentioned, what jobs are shown as the most rewarding, how are foreigners presented, and are there still 'job stereotypes' (the absent-minded professor, the weird scientist, and so on). In 1953 Dallas Smythe, in a survey for the National Association of Educational Broadcasters, analysed the content of one week's television in New York City, so far as the treatment of different jobs was concerned. Journalists emerged as the most popular profession, and scientists as the least popular; teachers were shown as the weakest characters and lawyers as the most crooked. Is this pattern still true?

To these one might add questions suggested by the B.B.C. for their excellent series, *Looking at Television*. Did we learn something from the programme? Has it made life more interesting? Was the programme just meant to amuse, and if so was it good of its kind? Did the programme balance a number of viewpoints, or put one across more strongly than the others? Did the programme tell the whole truth, or was there anything left out? Was it well written? Was the material well selected and were the illustrations to the point? What was the aim of the programme, and did it succeed? Some of these questions are fairly abstract, and in general one is safer with more substantive questions, unless the class is a sophisticated one. For the others, 'Did the main character strike you as real?' is a better question than, 'What did you like about the film?'

In dealing with particular types of programme, the discussion can be much more specific, and A. P. Higgins, for one, has made some valuable suggestions for questions on particular programmes.[1] For myself, when discussing Western films, I generally begin by telling the class about the real West; a land made up of many recent immigrants desperate for jobs and food, a few very tough and probably loose women, a land where

[1] *Screen Education Year Book, 1961.* The following pages owe much to the pioneering work done by this author in the field of television appreciation, some of which has now been incorporated by him in an essay 'Education in Television' in *Screen Education* (UNESCO).

fist fights were considered undignified for a man, the knife or dagger being preferred. Living conditions were deplorable and unsanitary, and life was usually 'nasty, brutish, and short', with drunkenness as the main diversion. At this point I might ask the class to write me a story on 'A day in the Life of a *Real* Cowboy', with readings from Mark Twain, W. H. Davies and R. B. Cunningham Graham to help paint the picture. Pupils can also be told the truth about folk heroes, such as the psychopathic Billy the Kid, and Wyatt Earp and his handlebar moustache. After this mild debunking, it is easier for the class to pick out some of the myths that have crept into cowboy films. Women—who often come from the East—are glamorous and Max Factorised. The cowboy himself is one of nature's last gentlemen; a man of leisure, who seldom seems to have very much work to do, and who has few material possessions. He is not interested in things like food or dress, but has a passionate interest in right and wrong. Bypassing any existing legal institutions, the cowboy usually carries out justice, which nearly always means killing, as a lone crusade. But this he does chivalrously; no cowboy would ever shoot an enemy in the back, and there is a rigid code about never being the first to draw a weapon. When he does shoot, he is fantastically—or even miraculously—accurate, and the people he kills die quickly and cleanly; he also has an uncanny ability to knock people unconscious when on the verge of collapse himself.

The unreality of this is evident to most pupils. Why is it that the cowboy is nearly always strong and good-looking? Are there no other ways to settle questions than by violence? Is it right to take the law into one's own hands? Finally, why are Westerns so popular? Why is it that at almost every television station in the world programmes dealing with semimythical events at a small period of one nation's history are given an importance above almost any other type of film? Perhaps it is because the cowboy film, as well as being violent and exciting, is a morality story at an extremely simplified level. Its treatment of good and evil leads, not to the usual imponderable questions, but instead a fast climax, since everything in the cowboy world is dealt with in terms of black and white. Is this why it is an escape for so many people? In old-fashioned cowboy films, the cowboy goes out and gets his man—his only obstacles being physical ones. Now, in psychological Westerns, the cowboy is often fighting against himself, and only arrives at the right decision after a great deal of hesitation; by the enthusiasm of their approval, children will show that they are thoroughly involved in his personal conflict. The hero used to wear a white hat and the villain a black one, very much as saints have haloes and devils horns. Identification with good and evil is taken even further in some of the more traditional films. Whereas the hero is always clean-shaven and simply dressed, the villain sports a black moustache and a silk scarf or jewel-studded belt. The hero is an upright man who strides down Main Street, should he not be riding his horse; the villain tends to slouch and is often seen leaning on the saloon fence, or abusing the barmaid, who is often tied to him by a curious love–hate relationship. The hero, however, is always chivalrous.

Robert Warshow[1] has put forward the idea that the cowboy film is an escape from an urban reality into wide open spaces, where moral issues are fairly obvious, and life is simple, brave, and heroic. It is interesting that when the late Senator McCarthy 'investigated' Hollywood, two of his chief supporters were John Wayne and Gary Cooper, both cowboy actors of long standing. Perhaps the senator was an attractive figure to them because he behaved so like a cowboy in real life. Complex moral issues were simplified (but with catastrophic results), he rode rough-shod over the constitution and the law to get his man, and spoke to his followers in direct and earthy terms. Is this not some kind of comment on 'pioneering' justice?

There are some excellent cowboy films, and many poor ones. Discussions about them are nearly always interesting.[2] Perhaps their chief rival in popular drama is the crime film. Again, these

[1] *The Immediate Experience.*
[2] See also some suggestions for discussing cowboy films on p. 84.

films generally offer an interesting contrast to reality. In real life, private detectives may do a useful job, but as their work is usually concerned with divorce proceedings, it is hardly glamorous. Crooks too are often pathetic recidivists rather than master minds with sinister nicknames. In films these people usually commit crime for monetary gain; the other acceptable reason for crime is usually madness, which is generally portrayed in ways very different from reality. The conventional sinister foreigner will also make his appearance in these films. All this is a good field for discussion, and once again the criterion is: how real is the picture we are seeing? Why do people really commit crime? Children are specially qualified to talk about programmes about juvenile delinquency. Why are people so interested in these programmes? Do the programmes show convincingly that crime does not pay, or is this moral tagged on the end to satisfy the censor? Do we ever see anything of what happens to the criminal after conviction? Does the detective sometimes behave in the same tough manner as the crook? (This is a very pertinent question to ask about some American series.)[1]

Plays on television vary from weekly serials, which may be of the 'soap opera' variety, to serious drama. There are points for discussion which can apply to all these programmes. Dr Neil Postman gives a series of questions designed to make every pupil recapitulate the play seen in considerable detail in *Television and The Teaching of English.* If it is a family drama, for example, Postman would ask: what sort of people are they, what are their interests, their economic status, their education? If they have problems, are they financial, social or political? Does it strike you as a real family? What are the values of this family, and are they good ones? The more children remember and analyse, the more they will judge. The danger of television lies in the passiveness with which it is received, which may lead to a dreamy acceptance of many of its values, some of which are dubious. Many plays suggest, by their glossy, glamorised

[1] See also p. 86.

approach to life, that the acquisition of material goods is one of life's exclusive aims. We all know that television advertisements have an effect on personal buying habits, so one cannot assume that the programmes have no effect. As the O'Conor Committee pointed out[1] I.T.A. forbids in its advertisements anything likely to be injurious to children mentally, morally, and physically. Parents and teachers cannot help being aware of these possible dangers in all other programmes, both on I.T.V. and on the B.B.C.

Light comedies can be considered as part of drama, and can be equally variable. They can be as trite as the desire of an American sponsor who wanted 'happy shows about happy people with happy problems', or they can be amusing and tell us something significant at the same time. When television began, it was thought that, as it was a visual medium, the funniest jokes would naturally be visual ones. In fact this is hardly ever so; ten minutes of a comedian like Tony Hancock in an entirely static situation can be funnier than any slapstick. At all events, comedy shows often run to a pattern that can be discussed in class. What are the stock situations and characters? Are they merely clichés? Why do we find some programmes funnier than others? Do the best programmes have moments of pathos or realism? These questions mean more when they are linked with a particular programme, as they always should be.

The category of light entertainment also covers quiz programmes and variety shows. Quizzes are often very popular, and one reason must be that there is often a large money prize at stake. The difference between a quiz and a give-away show can at this point be made clear. Is it skill that enables the contestants to win, or merely luck? Is it interesting to watch because it tests the audience's knowledge as well, and tries to bring viewers into the programme, or is it because we see people tormented and often humiliated by their desire to get their hands on a big prize? Does the question-master ask his question

[1] *Children and Television Programmes.* Published by the B.B.C. and I.T.A. July 1960.

directly, or does he coax, hint and generally become the most important part of the show? Some of these programmes are mildly entertaining and occasionally instructive, but for the most part 'they are good for killing time, for those who like their time dead'.

Documentaries offer a more promising field to the teacher. Defined by John Grierson as a 'creative treatment of actuality', they take various forms. They can consist of a narration accompanying an otherwise silent film, or of 'bench work', where the camera gets its effects from still photographs, to an accompanying commentary. One can see the actual event and have interviews with people on the spot, or the film can be scripted to include professional actors. In every case, it is the authenticity of the background that matters, and the relationship of human beings towards it, rather than any plot or performance. At the end of a good documentary, we should know about the people concerned, their habits, speech, and something of their personalities. We should also know about the situation that produced the events, and the way the one interacts with the other. There is usually a theme to a documentary, and this represents the feeling of the director towards his material; the class should certainly be asked to discuss what it is. The teacher can follow this by asking specific questions on the programme's content. One question worth asking is, 'Was the programme on either early or late in the day? If so, do you think it should have been on in the middle of the evening?'.

Violence

The problem of violence on television usually evokes furious discussion amongst teachers as well as pupils. There are two sides to the argument. One, which we may call the Freudian view, holds that there is a valuable cathartic effect in watching violence on occasions, for it may relieve drives which might otherwise be acted out in real life. This has always been the defence of the Feast of Fools and other Saturnalia in history, and can still be heard when people defend detective stories, boxing, and hunting. It was also held by Havelock Ellis, quoted in an outstanding article by Owen Reed, head of children's programmes in B.B.C. Television.[1] As a child, Havelock Ellis was faced by the most ferocious violence in 'penny dreadfuls', as in this extract from *The Marvel*: 'The gaoler screwed up the horrible machine until the brigand's bones were nearly broken, and he shrieked aloud for mercy, though none was shown'.

The effect of this sort of thing, Havelock Ellis writes, was

a kind of fever...it was an excitement which overwhelmed all ordinary considerations. My mother forbade me to read these things, but, although I usually obeyed her, in this matter I was disobedient without compunction. But the fever subsided, as suddenly as it arose—probably it only lasted a few weeks—and left not a trace behind. It is an experience which enables me to realise how helpless we are in this matter. If this is the literature a boy needs, nothing will keep him away from it.

It is obvious that many children regard violence and horror on the screen as a test of their resilience; the scornful laughter with which horror is often greeted, and the eager conversations afterwards analysing how a certain horrific effect was achieved, bear this out. Do these contain confused feelings of horror and enjoyment? (One must not forget the silent child who may say nothing after an experience like this, but who may have been seriously upset.) Most stylised violence, the sort of pain that hurts nobody and the sort of death that happens when another redskin bites the dust, is heartily enjoyed by children, perhaps because it so obviously has no connection with reality, and can satisfy aggressive impulses without hurting anyone. That is why discussions of violence which make their points by counting the number of deaths seen on television each week do not get very far, since 200 deaths in a cowboy film generally have less force than one death realistically or sadistically treated.

The arguments against violence on television usually revolve around a different theory of viewing, which Dr Richard Fox[2] has called the Pavlovian theory. According to this, behaviour is a

[1] *Screen Education*, 17.

[2] 'TV and Mental Health', chapter in *The Social Impact of Film and Television on Youth* (UNESCO).

matter of learned responses, and if pictorial violence is associated with pleasure and excitement, it might conceivably become a model for behaviour. There is some support for this view from Himmelweit, who stated that too much ready violence on television may retard children's understanding of its possible consequence. Again, Owen Reed recounts a personal experience which many other parents must have had in some form.

I have a grown-up daughter whose attitude to dwarfs has been permanently affected by a television thriller seen at the age of twelve in which the murderer turned out to be a midget dressed as a little boy. The delayed close-up which finally revealed that the innocent little chap playing with the train set had the drugged stare of a homicidal paranoic left that young viewer with a permanent phobia.

Both the O'Conor Committee and the Council for Children's Welfare made complaints about sadistic incidents in television films and plays, the latter in these words:

For example, the somewhat dubious attitude towards crime, that it simply does not pay, is one that is reiterated hour after hour. Moreover, if a theme is worn threadbare through constant repetition and all its possible variations exhausted, then it is likely to become a vehicle for a particular aspect which has an element of sensationalism to relieve the monotony. So the changes are rung by a shower of sulphuric acid over the victim's face, the deaths in boiling acid, or the blind villain slapping the blind girl's face.[1]

The question whether children imitate things they see on television is equally complex. Undoubtedly there have been some crimes or suicides closely modelled upon certain television incidents, but it cannot be proved that those things would not have happened in any case, though perhaps in a different form. Television producers often justify violence by saying that it bounces off normal children, and that no popular programme could ever exist if it had to take into account the emotional state of a tiny minority. Many experts, however, believe that a very large minority of children could be upset and possibly tempted by a violent programme. The Underwood Report on maladjusted children estimated that 8 per cent of schoolchildren need psychiatric treatment at any one time, while other authorities set the figure higher. Is one to face such an audience with programmes about crime and violence taking up

[1] *Family Viewing.*

10 hours viewing time per week, with 5½ hours of this time in the early evening? In America, where the delinquency problem is far worse, Professor Schramm gives the following description of one week's output from five stations in an American city between the hours of 4 and 9 p.m. More than half of the hundred hours he watched were given over to programmes where violence had an important part, and

in the hundred hours we are describing there were 12 murders, 16 major gunfights, 21 persons shot (apparently not fatally), 21 other violent incidents with guns (ranging from shooting at but missing persons, to shooting-up a town), 37 hand-to-hand fights (15 fist fights, 15 incidents in which one person slugged another, an attempted murder with a pitch fork, 2 stranglings, etc.)?, one stabbing in the back with a butcher's knife, 4 attempted suicides, 3 successful, 4 people falling or pushed over cliffs, 2 cars running over cliffs, 2 attempts by cars to run over people on the side-walk, etc., etc.

He concludes,

The picture of the adult world presented on the children's hour is, therefore, heavy in physical violence, light in intellectual interchange, and deeply concerned with crime.[1]

American children can see a great deal of violence on their screens; Russian children can see almost none. English television hovers between these two extremes; the B.B.C. tries to maintain a balance, and has issued a programme policy concerning violence which every director is supposed to recognise, and which is reprinted in the Pilkington Report. In it we see that children's programmes should not show family quarrels and insecurities, nor other situations that might upset a child's feelings, such as desertion or cruelty in the home, especially if these are shown in contemporary settings. Portrayal of injury, disablements, or embarrassing personal disabilities is also forbidden. So far as the problem of audience-imitation is concerned, dangerous examples of easily imitated devilry, like traps or sabotaged bicycles, are not to be shown, and weapons like coshes and broken bottles are obviously considered more suspect than rifles and revolvers (a director of a programme in which a boy used a bow and arrow was inundated by letters, many from hospitals with patients who had lost eyes

[1] *Television in the Lives of Our Children.*

from these weapons). Gross brutality by a 'good' character is discouraged, as are fights where the details are over-emphasised.

For adult programmes, which we know are watched by many children, the ruling is merely that violence should never be shown for its own sake, but should be an integral part of the story if it is going to be there at all. Even so, the bloody, gruesome, or vicious must be avoided, and the sound track should not magnify the physical impact of violence.

Owen Reed gives a further list of things that he does not like children to see on television.

There is also the heart-stopping kind of shock which derives from suddenness itself, whether optical or acoustic, which is as likely to be found in a nature film (e.g. a sudden big close-up of a bird or fish) as in drama. The most dangerous kinds of shock, devastating to a child's confidence, is the Jekyll and Hyde psychological volte-face in which a character of the kindly and dependable type suddenly becomes its opposite.

This, he writes, is bad, 'not only because it confuses thought and causes nightmares, but because it destroys confidence in the giver'.

Some people might feel that these rules are in danger of becoming unrealistic. It is true that we have been living with horror-books and comics for some time, but it must be recognised that these are a different quality of experience from that offered by the screen. Seeing is believing. It is possible to shut a book or to skip a page, but it is difficult for a child to tear its eyes away from some revolting spectacle happening in front of him. As Mayhew once said, 'We do not enjoy street accidents, but they draw us in crowds'. The Pilkington Committee have pointed out that the fact that people recover from shock does not give anyone a licence to shock them. Television and the cinema are the most compulsive of the arts; when watching them disbelief is most easily suspended; for nearly everyone, to see something is far more vivid, and at times disturbing, than any image conjured up by words or sound.

Himmelweit found that of children's most persistent memories of television 'nearly all of them had to do with violence, and horror and murder specifically had touched them'. Some of these children could remember a few really horrific scenes from *The Quatermass Experiment* from four years before when they were eight years old. This supports the view that horrific images from the screen are more effective than on any other medium; and for this reason television producers have a great responsibility, which they do not always seem to face. There is a corresponding I.T.A. code on violence[1]; pupils can compare this with the B.B.C.'s code and consider perhaps how widely they are both observed. There is a danger that the teacher, by talking about screen violence, will help to create an interest in it, but on the whole consciousness is better than unconsciousness; it is a greater danger for children to see this sort of thing time and time again without a responsible adult to discover what they might feel about it all.

There is yet another objection to scenes of violence that is hard to meet. Dr. Himmelweit has observed in eight-year-old viewers of Westerns that they soon cease to be frightened of the fighting because 'it's only a story', and they soon transfer this assurance to real fighting in newsreels and other documentaries. Obviously no purpose is served by children being protected from the idea that violence hurts, and that death is real and usually tragic. In a way, violence *should* be disturbing; in another way, children should be protected from wanton disturbance. This is the constant dilemma presented by television in so far as it is still largely a family show. Owen Reed writes, 'Physical revulsion is a response to be aimed at scarcely ever in television, if at all, and then only in the context of information, to bring home unpalatable truths like the consequence of a nuclear explosion, malnutrition, or simply plain human irresponsibility'. But for times like these, when it is an essential part of a programme, the violence had better be shown at night and parents should be given plenty of warning beforehand. Otherwise, although there is room for knock-about cheerful violence in children's programmes, there seems little

[1] See *I.T.V. 1965—A Guide to Independent Television.*

excuse for including it in mid-evening programmes merely for kicks. Habituation to violence of this sort could be dangerous; as Miss Telford rightly says, the greatest danger is not the soft head but the hard heart. We are back with the B.B.C.'s notes for producers, 'A sequence involving violence should arise naturally from the story, and should therefore be dramatically necessary and defensible. If it is inserted extraneously for depraved effect, it should be rejected outright'. Some crime programmes can make their points excellently without the often dreary routine of fist fights, where the furniture is usually the only thing to suffer any material damage. Many programmes fall back on violence to achieve interest at all, and its mechanical inclusion is an index of the poverty of theme. *Z Cars*, already referred to, had only three stories dealing with murder in its first long series with the B.B.C., and lost neither excitement nor an audience because of this. Everything depends on the integrity of the director; we see violence in the spirit with which he has portrayed it.

Triviality

Excessive preoccupation with violence is one of the most obvious dangers of television, but there are other dangers which may be less dramatic but are as insidious. 'Triviality', Professor Tawney once said, 'is more dangerous to the soul than wickedness.' This is the view taken by Richard Hoggart, who describes what he understands by this term. 'We are in a pallid half light of the emotions where nothing shocks or startles or puts on edge, and nothing challenges, or gives joy or evokes sorrow; neither splendour nor misery; only the constant trickle of tinned milk and water which staves off the pangs of a positive hunger and denies the satisfaction of a solidly filling meal.'[1] Triviality was one of the chief charges levelled against television at the time when the Pilkington Committee were receiving evidence; the committee, while realising that there was no such thing as a trivial programme in the abstract, gave the following definition

The Uses of Literacy.

of what they meant by the term:

A trivial approach can consist in a failure to respect the potentialities of the subject matter, no matter what it be, or in too ready reliance in well-tried themes, or in a habit of conforming to established patterns, or in a reluctance to be imaginatively adventurous. A trivial presentation may consist in a failure to take full and disciplined advantage of the artistic and technical facilities which are relevant to a particular subject, or in an excessive interest in smart 'packaging' at the expense of the contents of the package, or in a reliance on 'gimmicks' so as to give a spurious interest to a programme at the cost of its imaginative integrity, or in too great a dependence on hackneyed devices for creating suspense or raising a laugh, or evoking tears.[1]

These are useful criteria for teachers to apply to certain programmes in discussion with children. 'Trivial', of course, can apply to all sorts of programmes and not just those one can categorise as bad light entertainment. There may be pupils who will still argue that if people like such programmes they should go on undisturbed, however bad the programmes may be (this cynical attitude is also found amongst television producers). This brings us to the purpose of broadcasting itself. Should we 'give the public what it wants', or with Lord Reith, 'Give the public something better than it now thinks it likes'? One view runs away from responsibility; the other embraces it a little too eagerly. Once again the answer seems to be some sort of compromise, and the difficulty lies in drawing the line between 'Twelve million patrons can't be wrong', and Bishop Wilson's 'The number of those who need to be awakened is far greater than those who need comfort'. The Pilkington Report has a long discussion on the whole notion of 'giving the public what it wants', and all that this implies. No one will ever decide these issues except for himself; but the more people who are prepared to discuss them, the better.

Propaganda

A most interesting aspect of television is the amount of incidental social propaganda which can slip into it. This is always of such a blameless nature that no one has ever protested at this form of thought-control, but it obviously has its dangers. In an

[1] *Report of the Committee on Broadcasting* (Pilkington Report).

article in *New Society*,[1] Peter Stone describes how the sound radio programme, *The Archers*, was devised by the B.B.C. Midland Region, who felt that their normal agricultural services were not reaching enough farmers. The omnibus edition of *The Archers* now holds an audience of about seven millions, of whom about half live in towns. It regularly includes technical matters to do with modern farming, though these do not occupy more than ten per cent of the time taken by any one programme. It is done so skilfully that the audience never feels that it is being preached at. Dan Archer, the main character, will say to Ned, one of his helpers, 'Before very long I'm changing this system, Ned ... we'll go in for the herring-bone pattern for milking parlours'. To make the effect more convincing, Ned will not reply with eager acquiescence, but will be clearly bored by this discussion; so Dan goes on, almost speaking to himself, 'Anyway, with a bit of luck, we'll get a grant towards it'. This is always the pattern: every good idea someone may have will be opposed by someone else, but the people with the good ideas are trustworthy characters, and the people in opposition are obviously out-of-date or inclined towards eccentricity, so progress is usually made. On occasions the programme goes in for more direct social propaganda: Jack Archer went into a mental home for a spell as a voluntary patient. Such propaganda can occasionally be found in television series, particularly when they are about hospitals or the police. The class should learn to spot it; a mention of crash helmets or safety belts, for example, or the clearing up of some minor point of law. It is a good exercise, as it is one more way of reminding pupils of the social power of television and the responsibility all broadcasters have.

DISCUSSING TELEVISION ADVERTISEMENTS

In some ways the British concept of a commercial service is a model of restraint, since programmes themselves are not sponsored by advertisers. Thus we can avoid lunacies like the

[1] *New Society*, April 1963.

(apocryphal?) case of the American gas company that sponsored a programme about the Nuremberg trials, but demanded that all references to gas chambers be deleted, for fear that their 'product image' would be harmed. In the British system, an advertiser buys time several months beforehand; he has no influence on the particular programme which is going to be screened with his advertisement. Thus his advertisements are recognisably separate from the rest of the programme; the situation where the star suddenly steps forward and advertises the product does not happen here. The maximum advertising time allowed in any one hour is seven minutes, with an average of six minutes per hour per day (seven minutes is found only in peak hours). This compares favourably with the fifty-fifty arrangement suffered by viewers in a few other countries!

Rules governing the content of advertisements are to be found in a booklet published by I.T.A. entitled *Principles for Television Advertising*. They seem fair, but like all rules can be interpreted differently. For example, the booklet states that 'All advertisements must be honest and truthful'. It is true that I.T.A. now bans trick devices except when absolutely necessary and harmless, such as the substitution of mashed potato for ice-cream in filmed advertisements where normal ice-cream would simply melt under the studio lighting. Yet can we really agree that all advertisements are genuinely honest and truthful in most senses of these words? It is pompous and humourless, of course, to object to *all* misleading claims, such as 'High Speed Gas', and other obvious hyperbole, but if pupils monitor the screen carefully, I think they should soon find areas of reasonable doubt, and these can be discussed. I.T.A. has also banned all advertising that plays on fear. Does the class agree?

Again, the booklet states that 'No product advertised shall contain a reference to a special quality incapable of being established'. This is done so often that it is surprising to find it condemned in the booklet. How many uncheckable claims can the class find in one evening's viewing? 'No advertisement can be used that takes advantage of the sense of loyalty and natural credulity of children.' Although advertisers do not know what programmes are going to be on when they buy time, they do know that between 5 and 7 p.m. is the time to show child- and mother-directed advertisements. The booklet also states that 'Children should not be encouraged to make themselves a nuisance to other people in the interests of any particular brand'. Are these two principles observed? It is for the class to decide by careful monitoring. 'No advertisement should contain a claim to cure any ailment or symptom of ill-health': once more one is astonished to find that this common practice is forbidden. Patent medicines are among the products most frequently advertised; and an American journal wrote recently, 'Some of the advertising on British television would run into trouble in the U.S. There is a lot of patent medicine "cure-all" advertising'. It should not be difficult for pupils to collect examples of this. Lastly, 'No advertisement shall contain copy exaggerated by the improper use of words, e.g. "magic", "miraculous" '. Obviously, few advertisements could be shown at all if this rule were widely followed, and a more normal criterion is to accept an obviously exaggerated piece of copy only if the audience can see it is harmless hyperbole. Whether this is always the case, or whether people are genuinely misled by exaggerated copy, is something the class can think about.

These lessons may make pupils critical of television advertising, unless, of course, they discover that the rules are being observed after all! The Pilkington Committee found I.T.A.'s control over advertising copy to be less than sufficient; and so long as television advertising continues to play a major part in British public life, it seems reasonable to inform pupils of the present state of the law. If they find that the law is being transgressed, the advertisers may be encouraged to put things right, and more pressure of this sort would undoubtedly improve matters. (There are of course advertisements that are witty and pleasant to look at, and there is no reason why they should not get their due.)

Typical rates charged by the 'big four' for a 30-second

advertisement in 1965 on Sundays varied from £330 (before 3 p.m.) to £2,130 (from 7.35 to 11.5 p.m.). The commodities most frequently advertised were, in this order, food and drink, household and general stores, toiletries and cosmetics, tobacco, medicinal articles, household equipment, motor cars and cycles, and wearing apparel. More detailed knowledge of these transactions can be found in the *Statistical Review of Press and Television Advertising.*[1] Altogether £85 m. was spent on television advertising in 1963.

The appeals made by these advertisements do not differ in kind from those we have already discussed, and the class can be set much the same sort of exercises.[2] Pupils should also look for 'product patterns', where the same sort of article makes the same sort of appeal. The pattern might be in the similar vocabulary ('new', 'fresh', 'pure'), or in the recurrent image used with the advertisement: a happy family, for example. What is the appeal made by cosmetics and shampoo, or sweet and chocolate advertisements? Pupils should ask themselves which sort of appeal appears most often, and why. There are many different ways of organising these lessons: groups of pupils can report on advertisements seen at different times, or individual pupils can describe and analyse one or two advertisements, and put the results in their television diary each week. On I.T.V. every Monday at 10 a.m. all the new commercials for that week are screened for the benefit of advertisers and agents, and this can be used by pupils in various ways, and particularly to discuss any new trends. This list of 'Monday's Newcomers' is also published in the *Television Mail,* plus a description and the chief copy line, and can be used for the same purpose.

The values that lie behind many advertisements are as bogus as the sort of people who appear in them. As the Pilkington Report points out, 'The criticism is rather that advertisements too often imply that, unless one buys the equip-

---

[1] Legion Publishing Company, Ltd, London.
[2] See p. 41.

ment or the product advertised, one will have cause for shame, or loss of self-respect, or cannot hope for happiness; and that if one does buy these things happiness, confidence, friends will accrue as a sort of free bonus'. In the world of advertisements, where material possessions make for the good life, and kindness to animals consists almost entirely in feeding them well, it is interesting to look at the actual people portrayed. We find that they tend to be especially greedy between meals.

Occasionally, they appear to find room for the standbys of life, bacon, eggs, cheese, butter, and beer. But this is not a serious part of their appetite. By far the greater part of their time and capacity is spent consuming fruit juice drinks, bubbling and gaseous liquids in fancy bottles, and in those over-worked stomachs goes on, all the time, the relentless plop plop plop of fruit drops, orange drops, mint drops, toffee drops, wodges of chocolate.[1]

The voices of these people are often as glutinous as their taste in food; as someone once said, you can almost feel the speaker's tongue licking you.

They are hygienic and hair-conscious, and unless they are suffering from headache tend to be rather forcedly cheerful. Their accents offer an interesting view of the English class system. Do special accents tend to go with special sorts of advertisement appeal? Models in advertisements may use 'photo-dentures' to cover the gap between their front teeth when they give the viewers their widest smile. Children on television are no less abnormal, and a writer in *Television Mail* complained about 'fat sausagy girls with blond ringlets' and 'shifty-eyed, scrubbed and smarmy boys, elocuting self-consciously'. This gap between the real and the advertisement world is readily appreciated by classes at school, and it is one that they enjoy writing about. Titles I have found especially successful for this are 'If people behaved as they do in television advertisements', 'A dialogue between you and an advertisement character', or 'The advertising campaign that tried to be honest'. Sophisticated classes can attempt to catalogue some of the basic assumptions of television advertisements, in much the same way as the Council for Children's Welfare has done in *Family*

[1] Jacqueline Wheldon, 'Little Mass-topia' in *Contrast*.

Viewing. The monitors there found that since people earning their living hardly ever appear in advertisements, we must assume that leisure is the best thing in life, and work exists merely to provide enough money to enjoy this leisure. Nothing is said about work being enjoyable and useful, and little is made of the pleasures that are free to everyone. Serious illness never occurs; and sweets, cigarettes and drinks are the important luxuries in life. This world is of course not taken seriously by viewers, but one must not imagine that it has no effect. Although viewers may know that 'it is just an advertisement', these values can be insidious, particularly if no one discusses them in the open.

CLASSWORK ON TELEVISION

Any experienced teacher knows that discussion by itself can be of limited value with a large class. The quiet ones are often left behind, and many of the points raised will be forgotten unless they are quickly followed up. For this reason, many practising teachers ask their classes to keep some form of television diary. This is not meant to cover all the children's viewing, but at least to make them more conscious of some of the programmes they are watching (the very fact that the pupil will have to make notes about a certain programme as soon as it has finished will help reduce the deadening effect of the constant flow).

This sort of diary, which has been already suggested by A. P. Higgins,[1] and which I follow closely here, takes the form of duplicated sheets of questions which the pupil is asked to answer:

1. Date.
2. Title of programme, and comments on it.
3. Time of transmission, and comments on this.
4. Broadcasting company.
5. Director.
6. Writer.
7. Fact or fiction.

[1] *Screen Education Year Book, 1963.*

8. If fact, whether interview, reporting, discussion, comments.
9. If fiction, whether Western, crime, domestic, comedy.
10. Give an outline of the contents of the programme.
11. Was it convincing?
12. What did you like in the programme?
13. What did you dislike?
14. What, if anything, did the newspaper critics say?
15. How many hours' television have you watched so far this week?

As an alternative to the duplicated sheet the class might copy down these questions beforehand into a special television notebook ready for answering. The press critics are often not much help to the teacher, since they have far too wide a range of programmes to watch, and insufficient space in which to describe them. *Television Mail*, easily the best weekly devoted to television, publishes a regular symposium called 'The Critics', which gives quotations from television criticism during the last week. Although these are most useful, it is far better for pupils to bring the teacher a cross-section of all the newspaper television criticism for that week, which he can display on the classroom wall. If he is in the habit of promoting television programmes by advance displays, it is sometimes informative after the event to stick what the critics say under the advance billing.

A blanket television diary of this sort has its drawbacks. The questions are very general, and the pupils may simply go on watching the programmes that they have always watched, despite the efforts of the teacher to promote certain programmes in advance. A way round this is to devise a second, more specialised, diary, to deal with certain types of programme only. The class can be divided into groups, which can then be assigned a certain programme to watch and to report on to the rest of the class. Initially these groups will probably want to watch the programmes that are already their favourites, but soon they can be weaned away from these, and with the aid of a special questionnaire will be viewing programmes which might have been unthinkable to them before (always provided that their parents do not mind). Bearing in mind Mr Silvey's remarks about channel loyalty, already quoted, this phenomenon is surely one of the things a teacher can tackle, since it obviously has a deleterious effect on pupils' ability to choose between one programme and another. The appendix to *Family Viewing* contains suggestions for questions on specialised programmes, and pupils themselves will think of many questions they should be asking each other about these programmes. As an example, Dr Neil Postman[1] has suggested questions that might be asked about any family drama:

1. How many members of the family are depicted, and what sort of people are they?
2. What is the family's economic status?
3. Is there any clue to the family's religious and political beliefs?
4. What are the family's problems, and are they solved by chance or reasoning?
5. What values does the play put forward?
6. Is the family a real one, and do you know one like it?

The same author has suggested yet a third form of television diary, to deal with what he terms 'cross-media analysis'. This is simply a comparison between a book or a play and its treatment on television. Describing the same thing, G. W. Cutts, Borough Education Officer for Widnes, writes:

A most depressing discovery was the apparent vacuum in which children's television experience existed. Of 126 secondary school children in the second, fourth, and fifth years, less than half remembered watching a programme because they had read the book on which it was based. Only 29 had read the book after seeing a programme based on it, and only 17 had read other books by the same author. There is an opportunity here for direct school-television link. The serial version of a good novel (*The Secret Garden, Great Expectations, The Black Arrow, The Silver Sword*, are past examples for different age groups) could be made the occasion for a study of the original, and comparison with its television adaptation in class. This could be supplemented by a library exhibition of other books by the same author; and in this way television and reading could be brought together

1 *Television and the Teaching of English.*

and each enlivened by the other. *The Age of Kings* series on B.B.C. television presented a wonderful opportunity to both the history teacher and the English teacher, the more so since there was a fortnight between episodes, to give time to sketch in the historical background, and to read from the Shakespeare play concerned.[1]

No one would quarrel with this, as long as it is quite clear that this sort of comparison does not mean criticising the television production merely because it deviates from the original. The original and the television version must be compared in their own right; and with a good adaptation by the script-writer, and proper preparation of the class by the teacher beforehand, the class will learn a great deal about both media. Dr Postman suggests questions we can ask after seeing a television adaptation, some of which I reproduce here:

1. Has the main character been changed? Have the minor characters been altered or abolished?
2. Has the original setting been changed?
3. Has the theme of the story been made more or less complex?
4. Has the original language been changed at all?
5. How are the non-visual parts of the book, such as passages describing introspection or atmosphere, conveyed on the television screen?
6. How well did the book describe things that are easier to convey on the screen, like personal descriptions and locations?

This can be an interesting process, but it is often easier to do it with films or film extracts, which can be reproduced as often as the passage can be read. This was considered in more detail in the last chapter.

Teachers of English can always ask the class to write stories which centre around television, and this can be another effective way of leading into a discussion. A teacher can follow up a really good film or play by asking his class to go on from where the action left off. He can set provocative titles that are bound

[1] *Screen Education*, 11.

to get a response, however exaggerated: 'The day the television screen went blank', 'The man who was haunted by television' and so on. He can give them clichés, and ask pupils to describe in a few words the sort of situation they have come from. I have found these quite useful:

'Is this some form of blackmail?' 'Oh, blackmail is such a nasty word.'
'I am arresting you for murder!' 'Is this some kind of joke?'
'Does this mean we can never see each other again?'
'It's no use—we're surrounded.'
'I only hope we get there in time.'
'You can't continue this experiment, Professor. You are venturing into the unknown.'
'O.K. Let's go.'

Many such ideas came from *Screen Guide*, once published by the British Film Institute, but now discontinued. It was produced in the form of a large wall guide, with illustrations and comments, both very useful for the teacher. The pictures would be of familiar and less familiar screen situations, or stills from the latest releases. The text would ask questions, and include quotations from critics and 'show-biz' columns. Although the wall-guide is unfortunately no longer published, the teacher can duplicate much of its effect with the aid of his pupils. The class should have part of its classroom wall given over to a weekly collage of television items, which can be provided by the pupils themselves.

CONCLUSION

By now pupils should know something about the good and the bad in television; they should know also that it is not just the advertisements that can have an insidious effect. Though it is a visual medium, it is surprising how much television depends on speech to communicate with its audience. As in the case of other mass media, when the audience gets larger, and the distance between it and the performer grows, the performer is tempted to counteract this by pretending that his audience is just one big happy family, and that he is personally involved with every one of them. This leads to the intimate confidential television voice, with its overtones of affection and heavy sincerity. Things are done in terms of Christian names, personal greetings, and warm smiles. People in the audience find themselves being addressed, by someone they have never met, in tones far warmer than they would normally use for their closest friend. This seems to me an unhealthy attitude; it can make performers cynical, and members of the audience very gullible. It is simple to spot bogus sincerity in advertising, when it is used merely to sell things; more difficult to assess it when it becomes part of the stock-in-trade of especially bad mass programmes, often a camouflage for their badness. It is for reasons like this that so much in the mass media cannot be accepted at its face value; one has to ask further questions.

A television company once inadvertently screened a film that had been shown six weeks before. The telephone switchboard staff was reinforced in case of complaints, but no one seemed to notice: there were no more telephone calls than normal. This is disturbing; but if the film was as pointless and banal as many of them are, and with as little feeling of genuine personality, one can hardly be surprised at the lack of reaction. Working with pupils on television appreciation will not make them remember bad programmes more vividly, but might teach some to avoid them altogether.

Several magazines publish the weekly TAM ratings, especially *The Stage and Television Today* and the *Television Mail*. To begin with, the class's reactions will be very much the same as those reflected by TAM, but it is interesting to see whether there are changes during the year. After a time the teacher can check this; he may see some changes, but he must never forget that most pupils will not have freedom of choice at home, and that he can only recommend that they watch certain programmes. That is why discussion should normally start with the most popular programmes.

CHAPTER V

MAGAZINES AND MUSIC
MAGAZINES

There is no collective noun to describe the weekly magazines, picture-story booklets and cheap paperback books that make up so much of an urban adolescent's reading diet. Pupils tend to refer to them all as 'books', while teachers, if they catch pupils reading them under the desk, will describe them as 'comics' or more probably as 'trash'. Indeed, when so many teachers are concerned with keeping this sort of literature out of school, it may come as a surprise to suggest that it could form the basis for some extremely useful lessons. Certainly there is little justification in introducing pupils to literature of this sort if they are previously unacquainted with it. But this is very rarely the case; the average working-class girl, for example, will read up to two 'love' comics a week and it has been estimated that 95 per cent of British children still read at least one comic each week. So the teacher is left in a dilemma: either to pretend that something he almost certainly will dislike is not there, or to make a frontal attack on it by examining it in class.

That this sort of literature is pretty worthless, few will dispute; but the fact that pupils will often risk quite a lot in order to read it in class should tell us something about its attraction for the young. No one really knows why children like it; it may be, as one American critic has said, that the speech 'balloon' in the comic strip is the 'pretext literate people console themselves with for reverting to the atavism of picture writing'![1] At any rate, the teacher will have a much better idea if he discusses it with his pupils, and even looks at a few issues with them. This sort of informed discussion can be of great benefit to pupils, since many of these comics work at

[1] White and Abel (ed.), *The Funnies*.

the level of private fantasy, and to bring this out into the light, although perhaps embarrassing at the time, may also act as a release, and such comics and magazines may not be so compelling for them in the future. Once again, the best approach is to analyse the type of story and characters these publications provide, and by doing so hope to give pupils some insight into both the essence of such fantasies and their hold over some adolescents. This insight may not cure adolescent pupils of liking the stuff, but it might go some way in giving them some sort of detachment from it, which in itself might be the first step towards feeling really critical. As always the teacher cannot hope to succeed in this by providing examples of bad literature only; the best answer to a poor book is still a good one, and when he is discussing, say, war comics, perhaps his most powerful point will be made when he reads to his class an extract from a real classic on the subject.

Boys' Comics

At their most childish level, comics deal with very simplified stories where the chief characters are often animals dressed in human clothes, and bearing alliterative names: Korky the Cat, Freddy the fearless Fly, and, of interest to psychoanalysts, Ego the Ostrich. This type of nomenclature is also shared by the human characters: Hungry Horace, Keyhole Kate, and Wuzzy Wiz (magic is his biz). All these characters appear, or appeared, in the *Dandy* and *Beano*, where we can still find 'Lord Snooty and his pals' as well as that great baroque figure 'Desperate Dan'. It is a strange world, where kings always wear their crowns, and schoolmasters are never without gowns and mortarboards. Most doors are opened by butlers, while tramps still carry bundles wrapped in red-spotted handkerchiefs. Although there is much violence, it is not viciously treated. There is endless corporal punishment, either with Dad's slipper, or with a cane that invariably looks like a shortened walking stick, but it does not seem to hurt too much, and the stick of dynamite that is so often ignited never causes anything worse than superficial burns, usually on the seat of the trousers. The only objection to these comics is their overall triviality.

Slightly more grown-up are the comics that abandon strip cartoons for longer stories, again of a very stylised nature. The *Rover and Wizard, Valiant* and *New Hotspur* provide three good examples. Amiable clichés abound: school teachers rasp, naughty boys chortle, stammer or gulp. Stories centred round the Wild West, the frozen North, historical romance or scientific exploration, themes noted by George Orwell in 1926, are still going strong, and foreigners are still treated with derision—especially if they happen to be teaching French—or else with a pleasant if slightly patronising understanding.

Mr Geary's face reddened. He simply couldn't believe his eyes. A titter ran round the class. 'So you're the new boy from India', said Mr Geary, and a nasty look appeared on his face. He glared at the Indian boy 'How dare you come in here with your hat on!'
The boy's lips trembled, but he stiffened and looked the teacher straight in the eye. 'Very sorry, Sahib, but it is no hat, but a turban,' he said. 'My religion forbids me to take it off in company. The head sahib has said that I may retain it.'

It is interesting that this sort of story is so often set in a public school, even though the comic's readership is predominantly working class. There is indeed a timeless quality about these comics. Charles Atlas still advises his readers that 'You too can have a body like mine', and stories continue to make use of butting and smelly goats, runaway steam rollers, boomerangs, soda-syphons, glue pots, water-pistols and pea-shooters. There is an endless stream of stories about the Second World War, and Germans still cannot find anything stronger to say when ambushed than 'Himmel'. (English soldiers, ambushed in their turn, often resort to 'Wow'.) There is often a story about an animal, usually a dog of quite astonishing accomplishments: 'By Bill's side trotted Joxer, the young Alsatian dog which has since become famous as the singing dog of radio, T.V., and cinema. How was Bill to guess that there would come an exciting night when Joxer would "sing" about Old Macdonald at a royal command performance?' How indeed?

In sporting stories, the home side never loses, though faced each week by dangerous opponents. Victory usually comes through a gimmick: a centre-half known as the 'human hairpin' will head off any accessible or inaccessible ball, or by wearing brightly coloured shirts the favourite side will find each other in the fading light. Grins are rueful, teeth gritted, orders are rapped out and villains duly scowl and snarl. This sort of comic has a kind of simplicity; its picture of the world is narrow, anti-intellectual and out of date, but it is seldom cruel or obviously harmful.

Books, comics and magazines for an older male audience

Adolescents often share their comics with an adult readership. Still at the comic-strip level we find the American Superman, who chooses to disguise himself as Clark Kent, a journalist who, with his apologetic smile and heavy horn-rimmed glasses, reminds one irresistibly of the film comedian Harold Lloyd. Once in his superman costume he performs many spectacular feats; he was accused by the Third Reich of being a Jew when his war exploits against the Nazis became too regular and successful. This is an example of how seriously comic figures can be taken—even in war time. It is common for characters in American strip cartoons to have a huge and devoted fan mail.

Superman makes it even easier for his audience to follow the story by his curiously expository style of thinking. 'This earth fault chasm I spotted would soon cause a destructive earthquake. But these metal beams I've forged out of ores down here should prevent it.' These are forged, incidentally, by special forces emanating from Superman's eyes; the amount of magic he uses to solve his problems puts him in the order of Aladdin's genie, dressed in a space suit.

There is also on the market a whole library of booklets dealing with the last war, and conveying their story by pictures which carry a large amount of dialogue. The tone of these stories is often heavily moralistic: a typical title is *The Grim Game of War*. Usually one of the characters will make a major psychological discovery about himself, but not before many people have been killed with a variety of pain, varying from 'ugh' to 'aaaagh'. If the characters have personal problems, they will often be made quite clear in the first picture and caption, which act as a prologue to the whole tale. These booklets are extremely popular amongst adolescents. Where they do not deal with war, it will be with the Wild West; in either case the essential story ingredients are largely the same.

American horror comics and their subsidiaries are another matter. Here we have a strip cartoon world full of violence, but with strong undertones of sexual sadism as well. 'Comic' is a misnomer for this sort of publication, which caters for puerile power fantasies which also appeal to many adolescents and to some adults. Whether the story deals with crime, science fiction or exploration, the formula is generally the same: there is a hero who is an acknowledged or unacknowledged superman, a girl with scant costume and protruding breasts (known to the trade as 'headlights'), and there is a villain. The advertisements in the comics make the appeal more explicit: Nazi atrocity photographs are offered for a small sum, or booklets on deceptively aggressive forms of self-defence. Strip-tease pictures are also available. The more personal advertisements give a clue to the sort of person who might want to escape into a world of violence and pneumatic bliss: blackheads are removed, dancing lessons offered, small physiques aggrandised and pimples disappear for ever. Their level of wish-fulfilment is about the same: 'Now you can master mathematics'. 'Surprise yourself! Start playing your favourite instrument straight away!'

There is a fourth class of magazine, itself difficult to categorise. The cover always has a model with the usual exposed bosom, promising yet another return to the breast for immature readers. Some of these magazines, especially the ones printed on newsprint, like *Reveille*, *Weekend* and *Titbits*, are more childish than erotic, and have a readership of both sexes. The contents are a mixture of pin-up photographs (men as well as women), jokes, 'fascinating facts', 'show-biz' gossip, stories and features as likely as 'The girl who tried to clean up sin city', about a parson's wife who posed as a call girl.

There are other magazines that are more glossy and more expensive. They contain a farrago of short suggestive stories ('The astronaut and the call girl', 'Cocktails for two', and 'Come into my parlour'), cartoons, highly coloured non-fiction ('Modern art is for nuts', 'Pregnancy—its cause and cure', 'My death struggle with the 12 pirates') and features showing nude girls arranged in provocative poses ('The naked truth', 'Rita Mermaid', 'Sexy steno'). There are also suggestive articles ('So you want to keep a mistress', 'Around the world in nine bedrooms'). The reader is treated like a voyeur; the small advertisements reiterate offers of more 'eye-catching photographs'. This market is more sophisticated in America, where writers of standing often contribute to such magazines, and where there is a great deal of attention paid to male fashion and appearance. Summarising the advertisements he saw in some of these magazines, a writer in *The Guardian* guessed that the typical 'Stag Trade' reader would spend his day like this. 'He washes with a virile soap, squirts, sprays, puts or rubs deodorant under his arm pits, then shaves with a special soap, foam or paste, slaps on an after-shave concoction, then perhaps a cologne. He pomades and combs his hair, puts talcum in his shoes, and leaves to face the adventures of the day.' As if to compensate for the dubious virility of their clientele, the titles of the magazines are tough and rugged: *Male*, *Modern Man*, and more accurately *Swank*, with rather pathetic subtitles: 'The magazine for playmen', 'Entertainment for sophisticated men'.

Over 80 million paperback books were produced in Great Britain in 1963, and many of these will have found their way to pupils still at school. They range from Penguin Books to cheap novelettes dealing with sex and violence in an underworld or Western setting. Sometimes there is some confusion: Zola or Balzac will have the same sort of cover (known in the trade as a 'breast seller') as Hank Janson or Mickey Spillane. There is yet another way of selling established classics to the un-initiated: '*Alice in Wonderland*, UNEXPURGATED!' The most insidious of these productions, the sex and crime novelettes, are written by pseudonymous authors with names as tough-sounding as those of the heroes in the novels, and run to a predictable formula. There is an average of two sex encounters, well spaced in the book, and one sadistic beating-up, often of a woman. The hero is tough and unsentimental, and talks in staccato mid-Atlantic slangy sentences. Paragraphing is brief, vocabulary limited, and grammar frequently at fault. The girls, once again, have 'straining breasts', and give in to the hero as gracelessly as they are themselves possessed. As Richard Hoggart says, 'It is a flat, tough and tasteless world'.[1]

The most infamous of these writers is undoubtedly Mickey Spillane, who has sold 74 million copies of his works. There is a brilliant analysis of these novels in *The Popular Arts*, where the authors, Stuart Hall and A. D. Whannel, point out that in six novels Mike Hammer, Spillane's anti-hero detective, kills a total of fifty-eight people. This is the new sort of detective; teachers who still live in the gently murderous world of Agatha Christie must think again. The whodunit, where Sherlock Holmes, complete with magnifying glass, would spend hours analysing a foot-print, has been replaced by the thriller, where 'the act of pursuit becomes almost exclusively physical and often extremely violent'. Judicial examination is replaced by a beating-up, and the classic ending is no longer an arrest, but a shooting, probably in the belly. Some detective heroes, notably those of Raymond Chandler and Dashiell Hammet, still retain some sort of muddled code of honour, and operate in a world that is not exclusively violent. This is not so in the 'paranoiac universe of Mickey Spillane, in which the world is a dark, terrifying, and hostile place, where elaborate and deadly plots are commonplace, where no man is free of guilt, and where the only response to any situation is violence, violence first and

---

[1] *The Uses of Literacy.*

last'.[1] As Hall and Whannel also point out, Spillane's own titles *Vengeance is Mine, I the Jury,* show a *personal* interest in hunting and killing criminals; but they cannot hint at the sadism, cruelty and perversion which are not even below the surface, but there for all to see.

> The mystery writer's material is melodrama, which is an exaggeration of violence and fear beyond what are normally experienced in life. The means he uses are realistic in the sense that such things can happen to people like these and in places like these, but this realism is superficial, the potential of emotion is overcharged, the compression of time and event is a violation of probability, and although such things happen, they do not happen so fast and in such a tight frame of logic to so closely knit a group of people.[2]

This was written by Raymond Chandler, one of the more respected violent mystery writers. What he is describing is obviously escapist writing of a sort; the detective in real life has little in common with his fictional counterparts, and to Chandler, once again, he is either 'a slow ex-policeman or a shabby little hack'. But some escapist writing is very much worse than the rest. Once again, it would be wrong for the teacher to condemn the whole genre altogether; his job is to help his pupils to discriminate and select.

Girls' comics

A girl's journey through the world of cheap magazines is also marked by escapism, but of an emotional rather than a violent nature. She may share childish comics with the boys, but soon she will be in the strip cartoon world of *Judy, Bunty* or *School Friend.* Here she will find strong melodrama and stark confrontation of good and evil by heroines with wide eyes and blonde plaits, and lynx-eyed sharp-faced school prefects. There is a lot of self-dramatising and wish-fulfilment; 'The Silent Three' is a typical title, and birth marks, discreetly disclosed, can still prove the heir to an ancient lineage. In 'The Girl with Second Sight' the exciting new girl is 'ribbed' by some

[1] Martin Maloney, 'A Grammar of assassination', *The Use and Misuse of Language.*
[2] *Raymond Chandler Speaking.*

nasty fourth-formers. She replies, with dignity, 'To whom do you speak, evil tongue? You speak to one in whom flows the blood of the ancient pharaohs'. Although school stories are popular, the same type of heroine can turn up as an ace ice-skater, ballet dancer, swimming champion or even as an orphan looking after someone else's children. Mystery is still popular; and various pets continue to play sympathetic supporting roles to their ever-loving mistresses.

Recently many of the traditional girls' magazines have been disturbed by the arrival of the pop singer in this age-group which once used still to enjoy playing with dolls. Large photographs are now given away, and the horoscopes of pop singers are published for anyone interested. In 'Surprise Corner', a typical story, Sarah Starr steals off to a concert given by her singing idol Elmer Preston, only to find that her English teacher, Miss Fossiter, is in the audience screaming behind her. Together they make friends with the singer and finally end up in 'a very expensive restaurant where we had a super meal'. This naturally creates a bond between pupil and teacher, and the story ends with each reminding the other to send him a birthday card.

Books, comics and magazines for an older female audience

'If you're the sort of girl who likes dating boys, jiving and going to coffee bars, then these are the picture stories for you. Because they are all about love—the special kind of love that comes only once in a lifetime.' In fact many of the readers of this sort of publication are middle-aged women not mentioned in the advertisement, and George Pumphrey[1] has found a 20 per cent masculine audience for these love comics. In fact, lessons on predominantly male—or female-oriented reading-matter are extremely popular with a mixed class, and can lead to some fascinating and very perceptive comments! The girls who make a habit of reading these comics are often under fifteen, and a preliminary study has suggested that the most avid readers

[1] *What children think of their comics.*

amongst them are the more retiring and solitary sort of girl, who may have difficulty in forming personal relationships. Such readers can either choose a weekly paper, like *Valentine* or *Mirabelle*, that mixes its story strips with a few magazine items, or they can go for the smaller 'Love Books'. These run in many series, and for one shilling one can choose between *Love Story Library*, *True Adventure Library*, *The Hospital Nurse Picture Library* and many others. They give one complete story each, and tell it in large crudely-drawn pictures.

In *The Writers' and Artists' Year Book*, the stipulated requirements of *Mirabelle* are 'Romantic picture stories with strong emotional appeal to teenagers. Simple direct plot. Personality articles on popular singing stars', while *Marilyn* 'Appeals to young women 16–26, married or single. Strong emotional plots with love interest maintained from first to last. Happy endings essential'. The editor of *True Love Stories* is at pains to point out to potential contributors 'No sex questions or controversial matter'.

A plot that must be romantic, simple, with a happy ending and no controversial matter is not a promising formula; and the anodyne it produces is an unattractive one. The story is always contemporary; in most cases the last picture shows the happy couple embracing, and 'The End' tastefully surrounded by a heart shape. There are two typical plots: either a girl will fall in love with a boy, overcoming an almost fatal misunderstanding which takes up most of the story, or she will come to realise some simple truth about herself or other people, in the nature of 'Money isn't everything', or 'A bird in the hand is worth two in the bush'. Difficulties are solved easily and without complications, and all problems have painless solutions. 'The world adjusts to the heroine, not by any action on her part, but by a sudden extraction of the painful element. In the wish-fulfilment stories, it just quietly adjusts.'[1] Love and marriage are the universal panacea for everything, and the only sin is to sin against your chances of getting somebody. 'Girls are seen at

[1] Raymond Williams, *Communications*.

the harem level.'[1] It is not surprising that the engagement ring is the symbol most lovingly dwelt on in these stories.

The heroine is generally under twenty, with enormous eyes, and dressed in a way that is moderately fashionable. Her name is short, and often abbreviated: Jill, Joy, Val, Kathy, Linda, Jean, or Sally. Her job might be nurse, fashion model, air-hostess or designer, but more often than not she has an indeter-minate but refined receptionist-typist-secretary sort of job; it may be made more interesting than most by being set in a television or film studio. There is little in these settings to remind readers of the factory floor or shop counter. She appears to be of middle-class origin, lives in a flat or at home, and uses the daintiest expressions; her strongest oath is never very much more than 'Gracious', or 'Heavens!' She is more generous with her clichés, frequently seeing red, flying off the handle or diving in at the deep end.

The hero has a square jaw and regular Nordic features. He dresses impeccably, is tough, and a little older than the heroine. His name might be Mike, Terry, Tom, Bill, Dave or Ben. He will talk in a mixture of terse 'witticisms' and strange mid-Atlantic slang: 'Guess he made me realise kicking the world around isn't gonna be any real fun till you come with me, honey'. He may have a powerful job, or merely lots of money, from sources that are not mentioned. On the other hand, he may occasionally be a policeman or bus driver.

Very often the story will have a couple of bad characters who are very easy to spot. The girl is often called Vivienne, Frances or Rita, and she will have narrow slanting eyes and thin, arched eyebrows. She will be a cunning flirt, and flaunts herself to an extent undreamed of by the heroine. The villain will of course be a wolf, well-tanned and handsome in a flashy sort of way, with a Jaguar car and a cottage in the country. In this sort of story, the heroine always decides that the more modest boy next door is far nicer.

The settings of these stories are also interesting. If they do not

[1] Richard Hoggart, *The Uses of Literacy.*

occur in the boss's office, we must look for the nearest café, coffee bar or night club. There is little here to remind us of the industrial revolution; towns consist of well-spaced houses with generous gardens, while outside there is a wide area of surrounding countryside, suitable for tennis, bathing or rowing on the lake. Pleasant encounters can also take place at the park bench or on the quayside.

These magazines are aimed at an overwhelmingly working-class audience; this leads to a fascinating tension in the stories between the desire for escape into a different world and the need to be able to identify with the main characters. In one story, the girl lives in a huge house with a large garden pool. Her boy friend arrives fully clad in evening dress, and takes her to a restaurant, where all the waiters are dressed in tails. After an altercation he snaps 'Stop shouting at me, my man. I'll pay'. Yet the same character can say to the same girl later on 'Thought we'd take a bit of a stroll eh? Go to the pics and then have some fish 'n' chips'. Most of the heroines have expensive clothes, bedroom suites and costly jewellery. Their boy friends often have sports cars, and no financial worries. The advertiser who described these stories as 'Cinderella stories for a Cinderella class' knew what he was talking about.

There are also in these magazines horoscopes, fashions, and an assortment of 'wallflower' advertisements, in which with the help of supernatural or natural agencies bad figures, spots and dry scalps are rectified and beauty is at last achieved. Some of these are also written in picture-story form. Articles about pop singers are also to be found, and lucky charms, said to be worn by the stars themselves, are given away with a good deal of publicity at regular intervals. *Valentine* has stories 'suggested' by the titles of pop songs, while *Mirabelle* carries articles like 'The magic night no girl could ever forget', when Lynn Ripley went to see the Beatles in their own dressing room. Her impressions are in the same vein as the rest of the magazine. 'A cigarette still warm from George's lips, lay burning in the ashtray, while the strains of *She loves you* came floating from the

wings. Would they have changed by the time we met again? . . .
Dear brown-eyed Paul McCartney might turn into an angel.'
On the back page another pop singer, Adam Faith, answers
readers' letters with vigorous advice. To the question 'Could a
boy decide he wanted to get engaged after only one date?'
Adam replies, 'He'd sure have to be a double fast worker, but
I guess it happens. You must be some girl if you've got a boy in
a tizz that quick'.

There is quite a quick death rate in these magazines, since
they tend to fade with the pop singer they have been named
after. But they are soon replaced, and the teacher will find a
large readership amongst most of his girl pupils.

Fewer than half the middle-class girls will ever come across
picture story magazines at all; yet the average working-class
girl may read up to two each week. In general middle-class
girls copy their mothers and have a phase of reading the
glossy women's magazines, which cost slightly more than the
others and have names like *Woman*, *Woman's Own*, and *Woman's
Realm*. Although 30 per cent of their readership is working-
class the middle-class audience is obviously larger, and the
tone of the magazines is, for want of a better word, very bour-
geois.

One of them advertises itself in *The Writers' and Artists' Year
Book* as 'A magazine for women who want to get the most out
of life—whose minds range beyond the kitchen sink. We cover
the art of living—and loving'. With this recipe, it is not surprising that the fiction contained in them has a strongly
escapist flavour. They are an improvement on the stories in
the picture magazines, since they do contain elements of reality.
Often a story will begin promisingly: 'It isn't the big things
that destroy a marriage, thought Liz. The tragedies, the heartbreak only bring a husband and wife closer. It's the little
things: dinner at six with the children kicking each other under
the table; the evening stretching ahead; the talk, all surface
and without meaning; the flickering television; the barrier of
a newspaper'. But the confidence trick is nearly always the

same: having engaged our sympathies with the description of a real situation, albeit with the aid of numerous clichés, the author will escape from it with an unreal—even magical—ending. In the story I have quoted from, after some whispered and not very profound advice from a friend, the heroine rushes to her stuffy husband and embraces him. 'It would take her a long time to tell him, she thought. She had a lifetime ahead of her in which to tell him, watching him grow taller and taller until his head touched the clouds, his eyes reflected the sky'.

Serious problems, such as divorce or illegitimacy, are hardly ever treated, probably because the inevitable happy ending would be too much to take, even for an audience so conditioned to this sort of thing. Instead, the problems chosen tend to be real but superficial, and their solution unconvincing. Happiness is achieved often with the aid of incredible coincidences, or the heroine will allow herself to be picked up, with the most impeccable taste, by the archetypal tall dark stranger, whose cheery voice will prove the answer to all her troubles. If this time-honoured wish-fulfilment does not take place, the author will fall back on a mechanical solution, where suddenly all dark clouds will disappear, and what appeared to be a very black situation will now seem very rosy indeed. As Raymond Williams points out, the heroine has little to do but sit tight; the solution will always arrive, regardless of what she does. The most she may be asked to do is to adjust herself to it; there is seldom a more active role she can play. He also claims that this perpetually submissive role is also urged in the answers to the readers' correspondence; a quick study with a class could substantiate this if it were true. This line of least resistance somehow becomes synonymous with the femininity of the heroines: they are never very positive individuals, and if they have a career it is only so that they may give it up at the first opportunity, for the sake of marriage and the children. Any idea that there may be something wrong with society or a woman's place in it, and that she might do something about it, is always disavowed. In these stories, nothing *is* very wrong with society. A woman's proper place is in the arms of her husband or fiancé and her eternal phrase is 'Yes, darling'.

This heroine is generally described as 'not really beautiful, but...' and there is a lavish half or full tone illustration to remove any further doubts about her attractiveness. The physical stereotypes in these pictures can be analysed in class. Her hair may be anything from 'buttercup blonde' to 'deep red', and her eyes once again are exceedingly large and round, and varying in colour from 'sherry' to 'emerald'. Although the qualities are simple, the adjectives, it will be seen, are provocative. She is slightly older than the heroines of the picture-story magazines, and her name will also reflect a social upgrading: Vanessa, Charlotte, Anita, Alessa, Elspeth, as well as the favourite and universal Sally and Anne. Her job, if she is not a housewife, will be in the middle-class range, and her home will be equally safe.

Her man, once again, will have 'ugly good looks', and will be a little older than the heroine, living by himself, or occasionally with jealous parents, in a pleasant area. He is always tall, square-jawed, and has fascinating eyes: slate-grey, bright blue, burning brown or merely twinkling; when he smiles, or puts on his 'infuriating grin', they might wrinkle at the corners under their oddly but attractively shaped brows. He may have a tan, and a rugged if somewhat hirsute physique; he may also smoke a pipe. He may be employed in a respectable business, or better still, in a profession. Whatever it is, it will not be *too* exalted, for, as George Orwell pointed out, readers no longer want to identify with a duchess, but rather with the wife of a bank manager. His name will be as classy as his way of life: Rodney, Simon, Duncan, Hugh or Gerald.

In general these stories manage without villains; if some characters are disagreeable, it is usually made possible to forgive them by the end of the tale. Typical of these is the gossipy old neighbour, who may be a nuisance, but unconsciously will help our heroine over an important decision.

The settings of these stories make another interesting study which pupils will enjoy. Apart from the office, or some other place of work, classy holiday resorts seem to be a good place for meeting dark handsome strangers. It could happen on the quayside, or while swimming, yachting or playing tennis. Sports are seldom more proletarian than these, and restaurants, clothes and cars reflect a similarly expensive way of life for the single girl. Once married, however, financial problems are a recurrent theme, and many couples begin their story by being 'in the red'. Other popular problems are adoptions, parents-in-law, or the dark handsome stranger who makes a troublesome reappearance in the guise of an 'old flame'.

There are also 'true life' stories of celebrities, which read suspiciously like the acknowledged fiction published in the magazine, and awestruck articles about royalty, generously padded out with pointless banalities, and written in breathy clichés with the same mixture of sentiment and sentimentality.

There are of course reasons other than this shallow type of writing for buying women's magazines. Occasionally there will be quite a good story written by a well-known writer. There are other articles, on domestic consumption and children, for example. One women's magazine received 35,000 letters in one year on pregnancy and child health alone. Sections on cooking, knitting, sewing and housecraft are generally included, and obviously play an important role for readers who might otherwise feel cut off. But even in these practical matters the same gushy escapist mood is still apparent. In articles on cooking the colour illustrations often have an idealised and quite unreal look; as Mary McCarthy points out, the accompanying words may have a bright deceptive ring about them. 'Serve piping hot with a dish of wildly hot mustard nearby.'[1] She goes on to mention other tricks of style: the clusters of exclamation marks, the hyperbole of fashion reports (*little* hats, *vast* sleeves, *enormous* handbags), the chummy girlishness of the general features (*fun* with food, *terrific* ready-mix cakes, husband and wife *teams* who do *exciting* things), and the genteel eroticism

'Up the ladder from *Charm* to *Vogue*', from *On the Contrary*.

to be found again in the fashion reports (*plunging* necklines and *figure-hugging* dresses). She compares the tone of the magazine to that of a psychiatric nurse, and it is difficult not to feel that this glossy view of life, which shelters the reader while titillating her at the same time, is the magazines' main attraction. The style and outlook of some of the readers' letters often show the influence of this outlook. Such magazines rarely enhance life; they can, however, offer a few hours' escape, leading, in repeated doses, to a vacuously bright outlook on life.

There is another kind of woman's magazine aimed almost exclusively at the working class, with titles like *Red Star Weekly*, *Red Letter*, *Secrets* and *My Weekly*. They are distinguished by the crude paper on which they are printed, and the garish colours on the front page. The main ingredient is still endless serial stories, which must have 'strong dramatic interest and love interest to appeal to working-class young women'.[1] The tone of these magazines is quite different from that of the 'glossies', although the pattern of the stories tends to be the same. Recipes are simpler, illustrations are more old-fashioned, layout is cruder, and there is sometimes a breezy humour which would be quite out of place in their more refined rivals. There are a few strip cartoons, regular features like 'Uncle Sid's joke corner', or 'Our kids—God bless them'. Readers' letters, as often as not, are signed by 'Doubting' or 'Self-conscious'; there are more advertisements for patent medicines and corsets, but fewer features on domestic issues than in the glossy magazines. Items which are not stories are nevertheless cast in exactly the same mould: 'Have I done right by my daughter? A mother's problem', or 'Stories I haven't told before', by a registrar. Occasionally we may hear about a suicide or a murder through these channels; subjects that are almost completely taboo in the glossies. These magazines are more easily found in the North than the South of England, and they are a feature of the small shop at the corner, rather than the multiple newsagent.

[1] Editor's requirements for *Secrets* from *The Writers' and Artists' Year Book*

Classwork on magazines

Most of these comics and magazines operate on the level of personal fantasy, and although the teacher may feel repelled by some of them, he will be performing a useful task by bringing them from a private world into a public forum. There, they may prove much less compelling to some of the more addicted readers, especially if the teacher is at hand to offer something better. That is why the class can afford to spend time analysing the material in the way I have just outlined; by working out the invariable patterns for themselves, pupils will begin to realise how repetitive and flat it all really is.

The best antidotes to bad comics, sadistic thrillers and sugary love stories are of course amusing books, good detective novels and well-written stories. Pupils should of course always be encouraged to read these in as many ways as possible, but the teacher's job may be easier if he can give them a hint of some of the deficiencies of their present diet.

With comics, the teacher can very soon establish that the strip cartoon is of necessity a very limited and unsatisfying way of telling a story. He can do this by comparing a classic novel with one of the 'Classic' comics based on it. He can easily show how nothing of the real excitement or characterisation is ever recaptured in this way. Comics are full of clichés, illogicalities and impossibilities. They show a complete absence of real imagination and very little feeling for satire. Pupils should give their own examples of these deficiencies, and the teacher should read examples of comic-strip simplification and ask them to comment. When the class has had enough of this, let him simply read to it some of the best children's stories. Given some help and a little organisation, some pupils should soon learn to find and read them for themselves.

Tough comics and novelettes are a different matter. The teacher can point out from the advertisements what sort of reader the magazine expects to cater for, and he can discuss why some people feel the need for this sort of thing. A class should discuss the different formulae around which these works are written, and look for analogies in films and television productions.

When the teacher discusses alternative reading, he should remember once again that the best answer to a bad 'tough' novelette is not George Eliot or R. M. Ballantyne but more probably a *good* tough novel. It would be foolish to try to woo adolescents away from violent themes altogether; some feeling for this is surely natural. It is the degraded treatment of such themes that should constitute the teacher's chief worry. The same argument applies for finding alternatives to trashy love comics for girls. Some schools already operate interesting schemes for buying paperback books, or for having them sold on the school premises, while a few public libraries also have plans to stimulate and interest their adolescent readers. So long as these schemes work with rather than against adolescent taste, there will be some hope of defeating tedious semi-pornographic violent literature—which a teacher cannot hope to discourage by merely ignoring it.

Girls enjoy analysing women's magazines, almost as if they had been harbouring some secret scorn against them for some time. When the stories have been thoroughly examined, pupils can see which problems, jobs and character types are never mentioned, and why this might be. Are the problems raised in the readers' letters the same as those dealt with in the stories? The class can take a typical story and then make up a sequel saying what would *really* happen if the situation were a real one. The language used in these stories is also very revealing: stereotyped descriptions of love or an embrace can be so similar from story to story that one feels that a computer could have written them. What sort of language is used to describe the hero and heroine, and what impression is it designed to give?

In their folders pupils can collect the last paragraphs or the penultimate pictures of sentimental stories, and can discover what, if any, are the common factors running through them. They can cut out pictures of different heroes and heroines and compare them too. How do the chief characters of picture-story

magazines differ in looks from those to be found in the pages of
the glossies? Is there a social difference here? What particular
item of the story is generally picked out for illustration in the
title picture of the women's magazines? Is there a common
style for these pictures—a type of ink wash which puts everything behind a romantic haze? All these questions are easier
to answer if the girls can stick examples in their folders and work
from there.

There is a fascinating connection between some of the advertisements and the stories in these magazines—where the
advertisements try to sell their articles by using the same
sources of romance and dream. In *Mirabelle* one strip-cartoon
advertisement began with 'Carol always seemed to miss out',
while the last picture sees her in a young man's arms, with a
full moon in the background—all thanks to a brand of hair
spray. In *Woman* there was a full colour picture of a young
lady looking dreamily at her young man in a punt, with green
leaves forming a pleasant arcade overhead. The whole scene is
very reminiscent of some of the illustrations in the same paper,
as is the language. 'He says "I love you", and the diamond on
her finger silently confirms their love. In its rainbow flashes
she sees the promise of their future happiness together.' Another
advertisement in *Woman's Own* begins, 'Because you know he's
yours, when you're with him, everything's wonderful. And
when you're not, all your time is spent in plans and dreams'.
If the class can notice how such common clichés and sentiments
can be used to sell things, then it might begin to see the quality
of such language for what it is really worth. The only difference
is that in the stories this type of language is not used to sell a
diamond ring or a polo-neck sweater, but an approach and a
set of attitudes towards life. Once again, the final yardstick
should be recognised fiction, and in this case, the type that
deals with the emotions, but in a style that would appear out
of place in the world of advertisements. As always, the class
will be the final judge, and it is up to the teacher to see that
the comparison is made as effectively as possible. Once he

has pointed to the choice, it is for his pupils to choose. They will at least know that an alternative exists which does not have the weaknesses and faults of some of their habitual reading matter.

POP MUSIC

Every Saturday about £250,000 is spent on pop records. Teachers may hesitate before dealing with pop music, and all the teenage culture that goes with it, since by its very nature current music is not meant to last, and will be quickly forgotten immediately after it has been in vogue. Nevertheless, although the songs will change, the phenomenon seems fairly constant, and is an important, and occasionally hysterical part of most teenagers' lives. Much of this is due to the way in which young audiences and consumers are manipulated in the pop music world; and if the teacher decides that he will have nothing to do with it he is leaving the field clear for commercial operators, who are determined to have *a lot* to do with it. Teenagers spend so much time with pop music that ignorance about it on the teacher's part will also mean that he does not really know his pupils, who use this form of music as a form of self-expression.

Lessons on this subject can be fun as well as instructive (need I say they should never be considered as a substitute for lessons about classical music?). No teacher need despise the pops; there are few of us who do not have a large repertoire of pop tunes accumulated over the years and remembered now with pleasure and affection. Many teachers judge pop music by its worst aspects; by the same process many pupils will despise modern art because of newspaper cuttings about a few exhibitionists. There is in fact much that is good and invigorating in pop music; there is also much more that is cheap and phoney. It may be very difficult to decide which is which, but the teacher and his class can at least talk about it and come to some conclusions.

The words themselves are often the most dismal part of pop music. The title of the song is very important, and will reappear at different times in the song with something of the regularity of an advertising slogan. This means that there will be little danger of any teenager forgetting the name of a song when ordering it from a record shop. The moods of most songs vary each year according to the style of music, but *love* is the centre around which the theme and action revolve. Before the Second World War it was treated with a reverence normally given to religion as the universal cure for trouble and woe, rather as in the romantic strip cartoon magazines today. Now the mood is different, and the lyrics deal with problems as much as passion: the teenager is asked to identify with the tragic hero as well as the starry-eyed romantic.

Seen as a whole, love songs trace a relationship right through from its tremulous beginning to its tearful culmination. At the start, the hero is lonely, with no one to love. Stage two is the first meeting with the loved one, and is absolute in its certainty.

> Met him on a Monday
> And my heart stood still
> Somebody told me
> That his name was Bill.

The loved one is usually a non-pareil: 'The sweetest girl in town'. These songs exalt the competitive aspect of such a catch, as well as the joy of being 'in their arms'.

> I want ev'ry one to know I'm happy baby,
> Got a smile that's ten feet wide,
> The other day you said you loved me baby,
> And my heart just filled with pride.

Parts of the body most frequently mentioned in these songs are eyes, hearts and lips, and the 'tender kiss' is another favourite preoccupation. In an oblique way, these songs will often hint at a far more intense relationship: 'I like it'; 'Let's do it'; and 'It takes a whole lot of loving just to keep my baby happy'. As one modern song writer has said, the problem is to get the boy and girl into bed without really saying so.

Problems arrive, and some of the doubts the hero (or heroine) may have will be openly expressed.

177

> The birds in the sky
> Would be sad and lonely,
> If they knew that I'd lost
> My one and only.
> They'd be sad
> If you're bad
> To me.

This may actually happen. Sometimes the difficulties may be resolved.

> Many a tear has to fall
> But it's all in the game
> All in the wonderful game
> That we know as love.

At other times, problems prove insoluble. The most popular song theme now takes over. The hero admits

> I'll never get over you.
> I just can't keep it a secret any more.
> It wasn't so long ago
> You told me that you loved me so.

Now,

> All alone am I
> Since you said goodbye,
> Oh lonesome me.

Occasionally there is a mild feeling of hope in all this sadness, but often the endings are as lugubrious as anyone could wish. Tears are commonly mentioned in such songs; and in this way many teenagers can express feelings that they may feel inhibited about showing or discussing. It is no wonder that people who find it difficult to express themselves in words may turn to records to do it for them, as the B.B.C. programme *Two-way Family Favourites* still shows.

There are of course many pop songs with bold rhythms and vigorous words, and they may not deal with love at all. Sometimes the lyrics are written around a moral tag, in words which bear a distinct similarity to well-known quotations.

> No man is an island,
> No man stands alone,
> Each man's joy is joy to me,
> Each man's grief my own.

At other times the opinions expressed in the songs are more vigorous and self-centred.

> The best things in life are free,
> But you can give 'em to the birds and the bees.
> I need money,
> That's-a what I want.

Occasionally the words of a pop song break new ground, and raise the possibility of a new language altogether.

> You ask me why, why I love him,
> Whoa, whoa, dum de da de, dum de da de doh
> I'll tell you why, why I love him,
> Whoa, whoa, dum de da de, dum de da de doh.

Nevertheless, many pop songs seem to have unhappy endings, and pupils may like to discuss why they accept these in songs but not in films. Do the words matter anyway? Is it because singers prefer songs they can load with sentiment rather than with earthy good spirits? The teacher should get pupils to look at other branches of pop music, and make comparisons with 'Blues', for example, which tend to be a far more honest and less self-pitying form of self-expression. Going back in history, he can ask them to examine folk songs dealing with similar topics, or music hall songs, which tend to be wry and self-mocking just when the pop song would be most despondent:

> Can't get away
> To marry you today.
> My wife won't let me.

Although the words may not mean very much to a pupil when taken out of their musical context, they will enable him to see what sort and quality of emotions are dealt with in pop songs, and, in comparison with other popular media, how well they are conveyed.

The tunes of pop songs depend entirely on the particular fashion of music 'in' at that moment. They all have one thing in common, however; a basically simple tune against a simple background. It is the sort of music that can be appreciated and even remembered after only one hearing: you hear it even if you are not listening to it. Jazz—for so long the scapegoat for all that was considered dreadful in modern trends—hardly gets a look in on the popularity charts since it shares with classical music a basically complex structure.

This extreme simplicity dooms most pop records to quick extinction, but some of the best tunes have a habit of cropping up again and again in some new interpretation; the teacher has a chance to compare different artists' 'renditions' of the same tune sung at different times. This will also make a good introduction to different fashions of pop music. Current tunes are more difficult to compare, since they are completely identified with the singer who has made them famous. Occasionally there may be more than one version of the same tune in the hit parade, and again the teacher has a chance to make direct comparisons, although most of the class will have already decided who is the best singer according to loyalties.

A study of the antecedents of pop tunes is also very interesting. Many are lifted straight out of classical music, with Chopin an easy favourite. Pupils should certainly be given the chance to hear and comment on the original in such cases. Some pop tunes are clearly derived from other recent pop records, or owe their success to their complete identification with the trend of the times. One good criterion for judging a pop tune with a class is therefore to ask whether it breaks any new ground, or is it, quite literally, in a groove?

But a pop record needs far more than a good tune and catchy lyrics. It has to have a singer, who is either famous or about to be; for most teenagers, the singer is more important than the song. Just as with film stars, the singer, or group, is rechristened by his manager with an appropriately rugged pseudonym: Tommy Steele, Billy Fury, Danny Storm, and even Ricky Fever and Eddie Sex. If he can sing it will be a help, but wonders can be achieved even if he cannot. About one famous pop singer, Stuart Morris, who gave him his first audition for the B.B.C., wrote: 'Basically he can't sing. I didn't believe it was safe to put him on ballads, because he couldn't sustain a note'.[1] But there are many ways in which a pop singer can get round a minor handicap like not being able to sing. The record that is finally presented to the public may have been put together from over thirty tape-recorded performances. The recording studio will be especially equipped with echo chambers and other balancing devices which enable a small voice to sound big. If the singer still cannot make it, he can 'double-track', by recording the song again on top of his original vocal track.[2] In all this the singer will be advised by his Artists and Recording manager, A and R man for short, who is an important member of the managing teams that swarm around pop singers.

The most important member of this team is of course the publicity manager. He must make the singer into a star; and at this stage personality gimmicks can be very useful. In the case of Adam Faith, Stuart Morris decided that 'His initial impact—I thought—was the sunken cheek, hungry look. When he smiles this disappears, so I refused to let him smile on the programme. He did smile, though, one week, and the result was dire; it was dreadful'. Gimmicks popular with other singers quickly come to mind: hair cuts, clothes, stage antics and so on. These are often advertised in advance in the pop music magazines. 'Some of you will know that I like to leap on top of a piano at one stage in my act!'[3] This is mild compared to the antics of the doyen of post-war singers, Elvis Presley, whose act has been compared to that of a male strip tease dancer; it is difficult to know whether it was his voice or his pelvis that made the greatest initial impact on the American public. England has produced a few imitators, one of whom used to specialise in appearing to seduce the microphone, and often lie flat out on the stage in the attempt. This led to the

---

[1] Quoted in Ellis, *The Big Beat Scene*.

[2] 'A small, flat voice can be souped up by emphasising the low frequencies and piping the result through an echo chamber. A slight speeding up of the recording tape can bring a brighter, happier sound to a naturally drab singer or clean the weariness out of a tired voice.' Quoted in *Operation Elvis*.

[3] Interview with Heinz Burt in *Record Mirror*.

curtain being lowered on him in the middle of a performance in Dublin, and later sharp words in the pop music press ('Clean up your stage act, Billy Fury'), which seemed to drive out this sort of thing, though perhaps only temporarily.

Some critics see the publicity manager as the only arbiter of who or what is going to be popular. 'The public does not make a tune popular. Subject to certain exceptions, some flukes here and there, we know in advance what is going to be popular six months ahead, and the publishing business makes sure a tune it wants to be popular is popular by spending enough money to make it popular. So let us be clear right away that the public may get neither what it wants, nor what it ought to have, but what it suits the provider to give.'[1] This claim, by the secretary of the Musicians' Union, Hardie Ratcliffe, may be exaggerated, but it is certainly worth discussing. Indeed it is a key text in pop culture generally.

There are many ways in which publicity men can keep popular idols in the public eye. Magazines which devote space to pop music must be fed 'personal' stories, and pupils should read John Kennedy's book about Tommy Steele to see quite how untrue these can be, and how pleased managers are when their lies are believed. If the stories *are* true, they may also be incredibly trite. 'At Lincoln, Ringo had ear-ache and had to cut short rehearsals to go to hospital to have his ear syringed. But he was soon back and the trouble seemed to have cleared up.... That's it then. Hope you've enjoyed these glimpses of life with the fabulous Beatles.'

There are also fan clubs to be organised, triumphal tours to be arranged, and help found to answer the idol's growing fan mail. His record will be brought to the attention of all available disc jockeys, and the manager will keep an anxious eye on the Top Twenty, the charts showing the best selling records of the week. With a bit of luck, additional publicity may be provided by the public, free of charge. Fans may have tussles

[1] Quoted in the National Union of Teachers' *Popular Culture and Personal Responsibility*.

with the police while queueing for tickets; a headmaster may
expel a boy for having a hair-cut reminiscent of the star, or
some well-meaning public figure may weigh in with a jeremiad,
such as the clergyman quoted by Royston Ellis: 'Rock 'n' roll
is a revival of devil dancing, the same sort of thing that is done
in black magic rituals. The effect will be to turn young people
into devil worshippers, to stimulate self-expression through
sex, to provoke lawlessness and impair nervous sensibility'.[1]

Meanwhile other 'linked industries' will be quick to get off
the mark. If the singer gives a concert, the hall will be surrounded by touts selling badges, photographs and magazines,
while enterprising manufacturers will plug the star's name on
different commercial articles. During the Beatles craze, one
teenage market provider had 'sole rights on thirty-two different
items—from balloons, biscuits and blouses to men's slacks,
salt and pepper pots, soft drinks, watches and women's suits.
Six weeks ago he was toying with a Beatle Easter egg'.[2] If the
star is a really big success he might lead to a new clothes fashion,
which will also be 'promoted'; but on the whole the tie-up
between dress and new dance crazes is much closer, as one saw
during the exploitation that followed the introduction of the
'twist'.

Thus a star is made; if he is really successful, his name will
be inscribed on many pencil boxes and his picture hung over
numerous beds. Boys tend to react towards him in an imitative
way: they will try to produce the same noise as the singer, often
late on a Saturday night, and they may dress like him and have
the same sort of haircut. Girls react far more emotionally,
and it is probably for this reason that nearly all the big singing
stars are men. Girl fans generally become interested well
before their teens, at the awkward age before boy friends have
properly begun but where ideas of love and romance already
mean a good deal. The singing star offers a one-way relationship
with no problems. His songs deal with topics about which his

[1] *The Big Beat Scene.*

[2] *Observer,* 5 January 1964.

fans feel curious but also a little embarrassed. Rather than talk about their own feelings, they will listen to the star expressing his, and imagine that they can reciprocate them. They will not stop at buying his record: they will collect photographs, autographs, newspaper and magazine cuttings, and may join a fan club. The total effect is that of buying the star as well as his records, just as some advertisements make the consumer feel as if they are buying love as well as a packet of hair shampoo or cigarettes.

As they grow older, most girls leave the adoration stage, and transfer their affections to boy friends, who may in some cases manage to look quite like one of the current pop stars. It is noticeable that the older girls who are still screaming at concerts are often the less attractive ones, the kind who also read picture romances well into middle age.

There are other, more social, reasons for the cult of the pop singer among teenagers. To know all the current hit parade is to be in the fashion, and one of the most important features in coffee bars, which teenagers often take over and turn into their own youth clubs, is the juke box. In a film *Fan Fever*, distributed by the B.F.I., a psychiatrist points out that most teenagers who belong to fan clubs are well-behaved and clubable, the very opposite of girls who hang around street corners, since to join in star worship is in itself a conventionally social thing to do. It is probably the tumultuous reception and jiving in the cinema that greeted the film *Rock around the Clock* which gave rise to the idea that pop music and its supporters are dangerous and anti-social.

The audience at a concert given by a pop singer at the height of his powers is a disturbing but not necessarily a disquieting spectacle. It is true that many girls scream pretty intensely, and a very few get as far as tears and even wetting themselves. But this noise is less a reaction to a particular singer than mild mob hysteria and a desire to show off, since one can hear girls practising their screams even before the safety curtain has gone up, and long after the concert is over, preferably in the echoing chambers of a railway arch. It is an ugly noise, but surely not qualitatively worse than full-throated roars at the touchline, or hearty cheers at the Coronation? When a girl cries out 'I love you' at a grinning pop star, she is not merely expressing her real feelings, but also competing with her friends who are also calling out. It is rare to see a girl sitting by herself going in for these hysterics; it is almost exclusively a group activity. Screaming in the middle of a song is a more instantaneous way of showing appreciation than clapping at the end of it, and there was a time when classical music was interrupted in the same way so that audiences could express their immediate feelings. Although there is tremendous noise at a pop concert, there is comparatively little applause between items—nothing to compare with the routine five curtain calls at a promenade concert. This latter practice is certainly more convenient for those in the audience who want to hear the music, but we should be very careful of saying that this is the *only* legitimate way of reacting at a concert.

Classwork on pop music

The teacher must decide how he tackles the many points suggested by a study of pop music and all its side-products. At any rate, his pupils will be only too glad to talk about it. Even if he still feels diffident about the whole subject, is this an invitation from his pupils that he should really refuse? Once more, by helping his pupils to express thoughts and feelings, he may be leading them on to some sort of self-knowledge and discrimination. If the teacher finds that he is encouraging his pupils to find fault with much of pop music and its world, I do not think he should be too worried, although he ought to try to find something in it that he really likes. In fact, bad pop music plays far too large a part in many young people's lives, to the exclusion of many other wider and more varied interests. Despite the recent song

> He couldn't resist her
> With her pocket transistor,

there is something very disturbing about the conditioning of young people to the constant accompaniment of canned music.

Within the limits of discussion, I think the teacher can legitimately aim at lessening the *complete* hold it has over some of his pupils' free time, and can also take the opportunity of introducing them to other things. He may have girl pupils who do not really like some pop music, but who feel they must go along with it in order to be acceptable to their social group. This can obviously be a delicate situation, but the teacher can show them and their friends that there is nothing *wrong* with discrimination of this sort, and perhaps gently introduce some other interests.

Many pop singers broadcasting on television mime their songs to the accompaniment of their own record, which is played in the background. This has been common practice on I.T.V. for some time, but recently the B.B.C. has also allowed it, and gave as its reason that 'the public want to hear the record as it sounded when it got on the hit parade'. Pupils should be told about this, and should try to guess when it is happening. They can ask themselves which singers can really sing, and which need the full co-operation of the recording studio and its effects (FX, in the trade). Why is it that fans always want to hear the song sung in exactly the same way, even to the extent that minor singers are always expected to imitate the style of the big stars? Once more, is it the song, or the singer's heavily publicised 'personality' that is the real attraction, and what does this tell us about the fans?

As well as *Fan Fever*, there is also an extremely good film *Lonely Boy* available from Contemporary Films, which deals with the Canadian pop star, Paul Anka, who was top of the hit parade at the age of sixteen. Both films have long and sometimes alarming shots of audience reactions to a pop singer, and also discuss the whole promotional machinery. They provide good material to answer some of the questions the teacher and his class will want to ask.

Another approach can be made through the Top Twenty

lists, which are reproduced on the B.B.C. and in most of the pop music magazines, and of course represent over-the-counter sales for that week in selected stores. This is an extremely important part of the whole set-up, since the competitive interest in seeing a record move up or down the charts is as great for most teenagers as interest in football league tables is for many of their fathers. Teenagers often know the Top Twenty by heart, and eagerly wait next week's instalment. The teacher can use this interest by asking the class to discuss the reasons why each record is in the hit parade. One record might be the latest dance craze, another will be made by a current favourite, a third may be taken from a successful film, while a fourth may have something as simple as a good story or tune! The teacher can also ask the class for its predictions for the positions next week, and its reasons for giving them. This might mean that pupils will develop a certain detachment from the scene as they begin to understand some of the more basic reasons for the success or eclipse of a pop record. Something of this is already done on the B.B.C. programme *Juke Box Jury*, but seldom in a very enlightening way. An intelligent pupil might have predicted that after the death of James Dean there would have been a run in songs about juvenile death, and indeed there was. Winter generally brings a Christmas song, and during the year there is nearly always a new dance, a song about religion, a comic record, a piece of film music and so on. If a pupil can give an intelligent reason why he expects one pop record to move up, and another to move down, he will have learned something, and so will the class. Many factors will be involved, but if pupils can understand at least some of them, they will be that much more difficult to manipulate in the future.

It is difficult to find out real information about pop singers, but it is worth making the attempt. The class can use any material it likes, but the teacher should make it quite clear that he does not want the bogus stories and general rubbish that pass for 'glimpses into the life of your favourite star'. Instead, he might suggest some questions, and challenge his pupils to find the answers. How old is the star? What is his real name and his former background? Where did he go to school, and how old was he when he left? What is his weekly income, and how much fan mail does he get? Who is his manager? How many successful discs has he made, and how many failures? What does he really think about his fans, his songs and his own performance? Some singers are reasonably direct and honest about it all, while others make protestations of 'sincerity' that tend to be of a piece with the glutinous quality of their songs.

These questions can provide some fascinating answers. There was a time when pop singers often left school at fifteen, and were something of social rebels. Now the trend is reversed, and the backgrounds of many current entertainers read like school success stories. The pop singer often earns a comparatively modest income, since he may have signed a five-year contract with a manager in the days when he was unknown. Some impresarios buy a whole stable of singers in this way and may earn far more than any of their protégés. Pupils might like to work out which pop singers belong to which stable, and if we learn that a very successful manager has taken over an unknown singer, we can keep an eye on the different publicity used to launch him, and the general fate and style of his records.

No pop song is ever popular for very long, but though they all disappear at the time they are not all ephemeral. The exigencies of the fashion that created them will also destroy them, but some of the best pop songs are revived every five years or so for the next generation of teenagers who do not know them. If they are revived once more, they will become a 'classic', and people who profess to hate pop music will allow themselves to know and enjoy them. Exactly the same situation applies to pop singers. However much they were disliked by the cultural élite when they first appeared, if they can hang on long enough they will be accepted in the end by non-teenage audiences as 'great artists', like Frank Sinatra or Sammy Davis junior.

As with all mass media studies, the teacher and his class

are dealing with material which varies between the good and the very bad, and they have not got history on their side to decide which is which. This is a difficult situation, but a stimulating one, as the teacher will find out if he faces it. He need not feel afraid that he is going to turn all his pupils into sharp-eyed critics who will no longer be able to enjoy any pop music at all. It has far too powerful an appeal for that. The best he can do is to make his pupils more articulate and more discriminating; he will also be able to help them to see the whole publicity machine and linked industries surrounding pop music for what they are worth. When faced with pop music, teenagers are not really the hysterical morons they are so often made out to be; yet how much of their at times admittedly bizarre behaviour in this field is genuine hysteria, a deliberate suspension of disbelief, or a mocking self-parody is still impossible to say with any certainty, and makes a fascinating problem for teachers—and their classes—to sort out for themselves.

APPENDIX A
NATIONAL PAPERS: ADVERTISING RATES

Newspaper	Cost per single column inch	Cost per full page
Daily Express	£30	£5,000
Daily Mail	£22	£3,250
Daily Mirror	—	£3,225
Daily Sketch	£9	£750
Daily Telegraph	£20	£3,875
The Weekend Telegraph		
Colour Magazine	—	£2,700
Daily Worker	30/-	
Evening News	£20	£3,250
Evening Standard	£13	£1,200
Financial Times	£10	£1,760
The Guardian	£8	£1,100
The Sun	£11	£1,672
The Times	£12	£1,800
News of the World	£48	£9,000
The Observer	£18	£3,168
The Observer		
Colour Magazine	—	£1,850
The People	£43	£7,150
Sunday Citizen	£5	£450
Sunday Express	£35	£6,000
Sunday Mirror	—	£3,900
Sunday Telegraph	£15	
Sunday Times	£26	£4,576
The Sunday Times		
Colour Magazine	—	£2,970

(Figures by kind permission of *British Rate and Data*, Maclean and Hunter.)

APPENDIX B
NEWSPAPER CIRCULATION

Daily Express	3,981,110	Evening News	1,278,423
Daily Mail	2,424,810	Evening Standard	680,446
Daily Mirror	4,956,997	News of the World	6,174,640
Daily Sketch	826,440	The Observer	829,284
Daily Telegraph	1,437,579	The People	5,509,221
Daily Worker	no figure given. c 60,000?	Sunday Citizen	236,483
Financial Times	152,149	Sunday Express	4,186,525
The Guardian	275,900	Sunday Mirror	5,022,214
The Sun	1,361,090	Sunday Telegraph	662,030
The Times	257,922	Sunday Times	1,275,177

(Figures quoted by kind permission of the Audit Bureau of Circulation,
January–June 1965.)

APPENDIXES

APPENDIX C
NATIONAL PAPERS: READERSHIP

Newspaper	Percentage of total adult readership	AB	C(1)	C(2)	DE
Daily Mirror	38	13%	26%	48%	42%
Daily Express	30	34%	36%	30%	26%
Daily Mail	17	23%	22%	15%	13%
The Sun	12	4%	7%	15%	15%
Daily Sketch	8	4%	6%	9%	8%
Daily Telegraph	8	27%	14%	4%	2%
Financial Times	1	5%	2%	—	—
The Times	2	9%	3%	1%	1%
The Guardian	2	9%	3%	1%	1%
Evening News	9	8%	12%	9%	8%
Evening Standard	4	7%	7%	3%	3%
News of the World	41	16%	28%	48%	50%
The People	40	20%	33%	46%	44%
Sunday Mirror	34	15%	27%	42%	35%
Sunday Express	26	49%	38%	21%	16%
Sunday Times	9	29%	13%	5%	2%
Sunday Telegraph	5	16%	9%	3%	2%
The Observer	6	18%	9%	3%	2%
Sunday Citizen	2	1%	2%	2%	1%

(*IPA National Readership Surveys Jan.–Dec.* 1965.)

APPENDIX D
SOME ORGANISATIONS CONCERNED WITH THE MASS MEDIA

1. The Press
   The Press Council, 110 Fleet Street, London, E.C.4

2. Advertising
   The Advertising Inquiry Council, 49 Cresswell Place, London, S.W.10
   The Advertising Association, 1 Bell Yard, London, W.C.2

3. Films
   The British Film Institute, 81 Dean Street, London, W.1
   The Society for Education in Film and Television, 34 Second Avenue, London, E.17

4. Television
   B.B.C., Broadcasting House, London, W.1
   Independent Television Authority, 70 Brompton Road, London, S.W.3
   Television Viewers Council, 35 Queen Anne Street, London, W.1

5. General Mass Media Studies
   Mass Communications Techniques Division, UNESCO, Place de Fontenoy, Paris-7e

UNDERSTANDING THE MASS MEDIA

READING LIST

GENERAL

ABRAMS, MARK. *The Teenage Consumer* (London Press Exchange Papers no. 5).
DURBAND, ALAN. *Contemporary English*, Books 1 and 2 (Hutchinson).
HALL, STUART AND WHANNEL, A. D. *The Popular Arts* (Hutchinson).
HART, JUDITH. *The Big Sell* (Lawrence and Wishart).
HAYAKAWA, S. I. (ed.). *The Use and Misuse of Language* (Fawcett Publications, Greenwich, Conn.).
HOGGART, RICHARD. *The Uses of Literacy* (Chatto and Windus, Penguin Books).
JACOB, NORMAN (ed.). *Culture for the Millions* (Van Nostrand).
MACDONALD, DWIGHT. *Against the American Grain* (Gollancz).
MACINNES, COLIN. *England, Half English* (McGibbon and Kee).
MCLUHAN, MARSHALL. *Understanding Media* (Routledge).
MINISTRY OF EDUCATION. *General Studies in Technical Colleges* (H.M.S.O.).
MINISTRY OF EDUCATION. *Half Our Future. A Report of the Central Advisory Council for Education* (H.M.S.O.).
NATIONAL UNION OF TEACHERS. *Popular Culture and Personal Responsibility.*
NATIONAL UNION OF TEACHERS. *Popular Culture and Personal Responsibility. A Study Outline*, ed. Brian Groombridge (a shortened version of the above).
ROSENBERG B. AND WHITE D. M. (eds). *Mass Culture* (Free Press and Falcon's Wing Press).
THOMPSON, DENYS. (ed). *Discrimination and Popular Culture* (Penguin Books).
THOMPSON, DENYS, AND LEAVIS, F. R. *Culture and Environment* (Chatto and Windus).
WILLIAMS, RAYMOND. *Communications* (Penguin Books).
WILLIAMS, RAYMOND. *Culture and Society* (Chatto and Windus, Penguin Books).

THE PRESS

ANDREWS, SIR LINTON. *Problems of an Editor* (Oxford University Press).
AUDIT BUREAU OF CIRCULATIONS. *The Half Yearly Circulation Review.*
British Rate and Data (Maclean and Hunter).
CHURCHILL, RANDOLPH. *What I said about the Press* (Weidenfeld and Nicholson).
CHRISTIANSEN, A. *Headlines All My Life* (Heinemann).
CUDLIP, HUGH. *Publish and be Damned* (Dakers).
CUDLIP, HUGH. *At your Peril* (Weidenfeld and Nicholson).
DENNING, LORD. *The Denning Report* (H.M.S.O.).
DODGE, JOHN, and VINER, GEORGE (eds). *The Practice of Journalism* (Heinemann).
INSTITUTE OF PRACTITIONERS IN ADVERTISING. *National Readership Survey.*
JOSEPH, MICHAEL. *Journalism for Profit* (Hutchinson).
LIEBLING, A. J. *The Press* (Ballantine).
MATHEWS, T. S. *The Sugar Pill* (Gollancz).
MOORHOUSE, GEOFFREY. *The Press* (Ward Lock).
Report of the Royal Commission on the Press (H.M.S.O.) 1949.
Report of the Royal Commission on the Press (H.M.S.O.) 1961–2.
Report of the Tribunal Appointed to Inquire into the Vassall Case and Related Matters (H.M.S.O.).
STEED, WICKHAM. *The Press* (Penguin Books).
THOMPSON, DENYS. *Between the Lines* (Muller).
WILLIAMS, FRANCIS. *Dangerous Estate* (Longmans, Arrow Books).

192

READING LIST

ADVERTISING

BIRCH, LIONEL. *The Advertising We Deserve?* (Muller).
BROWN, J. A. C. *Techniques of Persuasion* (Penguin Books).
Final Report of the Committee on Consumer Protection (H.M.S.O.).
GLOAG, J. *Advertising in Modern Life* (Heinemann).
GUNDREY, ELIZABETH, *Your Money's Worth* (Penguin Books).
HARRIS, R., AND SELDON, A. *Advertising in Action* (Hutchinson).
HARRIS, R. AND SELDON, A. *Advertising in a Free Society* (Newman Neame).
HOBSON, J. W. *Selection of Advertising Media* (Business Publications).
MAYER, MARTIN. *Madison Avenue, U.S.A.* (Harper, Penguin Books).
NATIONAL UNION OF TEACHERS. *The Teacher Looks at Advertising.*
PACKARD, VANCE. *The Hidden Persuaders* (David McKay, Penguin Books).
SMITH, G. H. *Motivational Research in Advertising* (McGraw-Hill).
THOMPSON, DENYS. *Voices of Civilisation* (Muller).
TUNSTALL, JEREMY. *The Advertising Man in London Advertising Agencies* (Chapman and Hall).
TURNER, E. S. *The Shocking History of Advertising* (Michael Joseph).
Teachers may also find the *Advertiser's Weekly* and the *World Press News* useful. The monthly publication of the Advertising Inquiry Council, *Scrutiny*, is no longer being issued, although there are hopes in the future to bring it out as a quarterly magazine. Meanwhile, Chatto and Windus are publishing a quarterly series of useful and attractive exercise sheets for schools called *Looking at Advertising*, at 4/6 per dozen. Also recommended are the monthly *Which*, published by the Consumers Association, and the monthly *Focus*, published by the Consumer Council.

FILMS

BRITISH FILM INSTITUTE. *Film and Television in Education for Teaching.*
FENIN, G., AND EVERSON, W. *The Western* (Orion Press, New York).
GOODMAN, EZRA. *The Fifty-Year Decline and Fall of Hollywood* (Simon and Schuster, New York).
GREINER, GRACE. *Teaching Film* (British Film Institute).
HARDY, F. *Grierson on Documentary* (Collins).
HODGKINSON, A. W. *Screen Education. Teaching a critical approach to cinema and television* (UNESCO).
HOUSTON, PENELOPE. *The Contemporary Cinema* (Penguin Books).
KNIGHT, ARTHUR. *The Liveliest Art* (Macmillan, New York).
LACLOS, M. *Le fantastique au Cinema* (Jean-Jacques Pauvert).
LINDGREN, ERNEST. *The Art of the Film* (Allen and Unwin).
MANVELL, ROGER. *Film* (Penguin Books).
MANVELL, ROGER. *The Film and the Public* (Penguin Books).
MONTAGUE, IVOR. *Film World* (Penguin Books).
MORIN, EDGAR. *The Stars* (John Calder).
REISZ, KAREL. *The Technique of Film Editing* (Focal Press)
RICE, ELMER. *Voyage to Purilia* (Penguin Books).
RICHARDSON, A. (ed). *A Handbook for Screen Education* (S.E.F.T. Publications).
ROSS, LILLIAN. *Picture* (Gollancz, Penguin Books).
SPRAOS, J. *The Decline of the Cinema* (Allen and Unwin).
TALBOT, D. *Film, an Anthology* (Simon and Schuster, New York).
VANNOEY, R. C. *Film Society Handbook* (S.E.F.T. Publications)
WARSHOW, A. D. *The Immediate Experience* (Doubleday, New York).

WHANNEL, P. (ed.). *Film Teaching* (British Film Institute).
The Wheare Report (H.M.S.O.).
ZINSSER, W. K. *Seen any Good Films Lately?* (Hammond, Hammond).
Teachers will also find the bi-monthly *Screen Education* and the *Screen Education Year Book*, (formerly *Film Teacher's Handbook*) both published by the S.E.F.T., more than useful. Also recommended are the quarterly *Sight and Sound*, published by the B.F.I., and *Film and Filming*, published every month by Hansom books, 16 Buckingham Palace Road, London, S.W.1.

Film Making

ALDER, R. H. *Movie-Making for Everyone* (Fountain Press).
ANKERSMITT, K. S. *Beginner's Guide to Ciné Photography* (Newnes).
BOMBACK, R. H. *Handbook of Amateur Cinematography* (Fountain Press).
CROYDON, JOHN. *Editing and Titling* (Fountain Press).
DAVIS, DENYS. *Filming Indoors* (Fountain Press).
DAVIS, DENYS. *Filming with 16 mm.* (Iliffe).
LARSEN, EGON. *Film Making* (Muller).
ROSE, TONY. *Simple Art of Making Films* (Focal Press).
WATERS, DON, AND REES, SYDNEY. *Young Film Makers* (S.E.F.T. Publications).
WILLS, B. H. R. (ed). *Young Film Makers Symposium* (S.E.F.T. Publications).

TELEVISION

BUSSEL, J. *The Art of Television* (Faber).
COUNCIL FOR CHILDREN'S WELFARE (M. Masheder, A. Holme, A. Higgins). *Family Viewing.*
CROZIER, MARY. *Broadcasting in Sound and Television* (Oxford University Press).
DAVIS, D. *Grammar of Television Production* (Barrie).
GRANADA T.V. *What Children Watch.*
GRANADA T.V. *Dons or Crooners?*
HIMMELWEIT, H., OPPENHEIM A. AND VINCE, P. *Television and the Child* (Oxford University Press).
JENKINS, CLIVE. *Power behind the Screen* (McGibbon and Kee).
LEVIN, RICHARD. *Television by Design* (Bodley Head).
O'CONOR, M., et al. *Children and Television Programmes* (B.B.C. and I.T.A.).
Parents, Children and Television (H.M.S.O.).
PAULU, B. *British Broadcasting in Transition* (Macmillan).
POSTMAN, N. *Television and the Teaching of English* (Appleton-Century-Crofts).
Report of the Committee on Broadcasting (Pilkington Report) (H.M.S.O.).
SCHRAMM, W. *Television in the Lives of Our Children* (Oxford).
SWINSON, ARTHUR. *Writing for Television* (Black).
TAYLOR, J. R. *Anatomy of a Television Play* (Weidenfeld and Nicholson).
TRENEMAN, J., AND McQUAIL, D. *Television and the Political Image* (Methuen).
UNESCO. *The Social Impact of Film and Television on Youth.*
WILSON, H. *Pressure Group* (Secker and Warburg).
Also recommended is the fortnightly *Television Mail*, and the annual reports of the B.B.C. and I.T.V.

COMICS AND MAGAZINES

GARDINER, D. AND WALKER, K. S. (eds). *Raymond Chandler Speaking* (Hamish Hamilton).
GRIEVE, MARY. *Millions Made My Story* (Gollancz).
McCARTHY, MARY. *On the Contrary* (Heinemann).

READING LIST

ORWELL, GEORGE. *Critical Essays* (Secker and Warburg).
PUMPHREY, G. *Children's Comics* (Epworth Press).
PUMPHREY, G. *What Children Think of their Comics* (Epworth Press).
TURNER, E. S. *Boys will be Boys* (Michael Joseph).
WAGNER, G. *Parade of Pleasure* (Verschoyle).
WERTHAM, F. *Seduction of the Innocent* (Museum Press).
WHITE, D. M., AND ABEL, R. H. (eds). *The Funnies* (Collier-Macmillan, London).
The Writers' and Artists' Year Book (Black).

POP MUSIC

ADLER, BILL. *Love Letters to the Beatles* (Anthony Blond).
BRAUN, MICHAEL. *Love Me Do* (Penguin Books).
ELLIS, ROYSTON. *The Big Beat Scene* (Four Square Books).
FAITH, ADAM. *Poor Me* (Four Square Books).
GAMMOND, P. AND CLAYTON, P. *A Guide to Popular Music* (Phoenix House).
KENNEDY, JOHN. *Tommy Steele* (Corgi Books).
LEVY, ALAN. *Operation Elvis* (Deutsch).
MURRAY, MITCH. *How to Write a Popular Song* (B. Feldman).
RICHARD, CLIFF, AND FERRIER, BOB. *The Wonderful World of Cliff Richard* (Davies).
ROGERS, E. *Tin Pan Alley* (Hale).
ROLLING STONES, THE. *Our Own Story* (Corgi Books).
The weekly *New Musical Express*, *New Record Mirror* and *Melody Maker* all have their uses for the teacher.

INDEX

Printed in the United States
149524LV00002B/11/P

9 780521 111966